The Handbook of
CHINESE
MASSAGE

The Handbook of
CHINESE
MASSAGE

Tui Na Techniques
to Awaken Body and Mind

MARIA MERCATI

Healing Arts Press
Rochester, Vermont

Healing Arts Press
One Park Street
Rochester, Vermont 05767
www.gotoit.com

This Healing Arts Press edition published in agreement with Gaia Books Limited 1997

First published in the United Kingdom under the title *Step-by-Step Tui Na: Massage to Awaken Body and Mind* by Gaia Books Limited 1997

Note to the reader: This book is intended as an informational guide. The remedies, approaches, and techniques described herein are meant to supplement, and not to be a substitute for, professional medical care or treatment. They should not be used to treat a serious ailment without prior consultation with a qualified health-care professional.

Library of Congress Cataloging-in-Publication Data

Mercati, Maria.
    The handbook of Chinese massage : Tuina techniques to awaken body and mind /
Maria Mercati.
      p.   cm.
    Includes bibliographical references and index.
    ISBN 0-89281-745-3 (alk. paper)
    1. Massage—China—Handbooks, manuals, etc.   I. Title.
RM723.C5M47 1997   97-17132
615.8'22—dc21   CIP

Printed in Italy

10 9 8 7 6 5 4 3 2

Healing Arts Press is a division of Inner Traditions International

Note on safety

The techniques and treatments in this book are to be used at the reader's sole discretion and risk. Always observe the cautions given, and consult a doctor if you are in any doubt about a medical condition.

Tui Na is very safe when performed according to the advice given in this book. One of its major applications is in relieving chronic pain, but it can also be used to treat a wide range of common ailments. As with any form of deep massage, Tui Na should not be practised on anyone suffering from cancer, severe heart disease, or osteoporosis. A full list of contraindications is given on page 12. Some of the treatments should not be used during pregnancy; wherever these are recommended they are highlighted with a caution printed in **bold**.

Contents

A note from the author

I discovered Tui Na during my own personal quest for a therapy to relieve crippling pain. As a child I suffered from a degenerative disease which affected my hip. As the years went by, standing and walking even for short distances caused me pain.

Whilst living in Indonesia for four years, I discovered the healing powers of deep Oriental massage, and trained as a massage therapist. Back in England and cut off from the weekly therapy that kept me mobile, my condition worsened. I tried many therapies, but without success. Western medicine could only offer me painkillers and a hip replacement operation. But instead of going to hospital for surgery, I travelled to China to learn Tui Na.

The skilful, patient doctors of Traditional Medicine gave me the treatment and tuition that I needed and opened a wonderful new chapter in my life.

At that time few people in the West had heard of Tui Na, although acupuncture and herbal medicine were available. So extraordinary was Tui Na's effect on me, it became my mission in life to bring it within reach of everyone in the West. I studied, worked, and travelled back to China time and again, to learn Tui Na and acupuncture from Chinese doctors in hospitals and clinics in Shanghai, Weihai, and X'ian.

I needed almost daily Tui Na treatment to keep myself pain-free, mobile, and able to work. My family grew increasingly interested in this system of healing, which they could see worked wonderfully on me and kept them full of energy, enthusiasm, and vitality. I trained my husband, my three daughters, and my son in the techniques of Tui Na so that they could give me treatment and it became a large part of their lives as it has mine. My elder daughters are now qualified therapists working in London, and my husband and son work with me at the BODYHARMONICS® Centre that we have established in Cheltenham.

There is growing interest in medical circles for more information on Tui Na and other forms of Traditional Chinese Medicine, and demand from educational and training bodies for a systematic training. In response to these demands I established the teaching side of the BODYHARMONICS® Centre, where we run regular training courses.

I have treated many people with disabling conditions that other forms of medicine could do little to help and have found that there is a real alternative to living on painkillers or having surgery. Tui Na has changed my life and the lives of many of my patients. I hope that it can do the same for you.

Maria Mercati

How to use this book

The Handbook of Chinese Massage gives a comprehensive introduction to the use of this ancient healing art of deep massage and manipulation. Accessible for readers who have no previous experience of massage therapies, its clear approach is also valuable for those trained in other forms of bodywork, or in Traditional Chinese Medicine.

Chapters One and Two describe the unique features of Tui Na and explain its roots in the 4000-year-old system of Traditional Chinese Medicine. These chapters give important background information for the more practical techniques that follow in the remaining chapters. Chapter Three uses illustrations and descriptions to show the energy pathways in the body, and points where this energy can be manipulated. You need to familiarize yourself with these and practise the Tui Na techniques for soft tissue massage and joint manipulations described in Chapter Four, before going on to giving the treatments described in the last two chapters.

The whole-body routine in Chapter Five is a unique holistic treatment, developed by the author. Focusing on each part of the body in turn, it restores balance in the body's energies, for health and wellbeing in body, mind, and spirit. Once you have mastered the techniques and learnt how to give the whole-body treatment, you can modify it, if necessary, to meet your partner's needs.

Chapter Six presents treatments for a variety of common conditions and ailments. One section is devoted to sports injuries, such as sprains and muscle strains, which can be treated very successfully using Tui Na. There are also treatments appropriate for infants, adolescents, and the elderly.

Tui Na is part of a medical system of healing, and for accuracy its techniques and applications have to be explained using medical anatomical terms. These are explained in the Appendix, which includes diagrams of the bones and muscles in the body, and a Glossary.

Many anatomical terms, such as the names of the organs of the body, have a wider meaning in Chinese medicine than they do in the West (see page 16). In this book the Chinese interpretation is indicated with an initial capital letter.

Tui Na for everyone

Tui Na is practised throughout China on people from the age of five upward. Babies and younger children are treated differently, since their Meridian systems are not fully developed. It is a very safe therapy: if pressure is applied in the wrong place, for example, there will be no beneficial result, and possibly a bruise, but no serious harm will be done. Qi-flow naturally rebalances itself in time.

Massage treatment of any form is not suitable for people with certain serious health conditions. These are listed above, right. In this book, wherever a treatment described is contraindicated for certain conditions, this is highlighted with a Caution note.

Tui Na is particularly effective in treating pain of the muscles and joints resulting from sports injury, wear and tear, chronic stress, or any other cause. It is also excellent for treating stress-related disorders. All massage therapies aid relaxation, but in addition to relaxing the muscles Tui Na also manipulates Qi-flow to balance the underlying energy problems which are associated with the stress. Many chronic conditions, such as irritable bowel syndrome, are aggravated by stress and can be greatly relieved by the deep massage techniques of Tui Na applied to specific points. As well as being an effective treatment for a variety of specific ailments and conditions, Tui Na also boosts vitality and wellbeing, which in turn stimulates the immune system and improves general health.

This book shows you useful techniques to help relieve pain and the symptoms of many common ailments. However, it does not replace professional health care and you should always consult a qualified practitioner or doctor if symptoms persist.

WHEN NOT TO USE TUI NA

● Tui Na is not suitable for those with serious heart disease or cancer, especially of the skin or lymphatic system.
● Do not massage anyone with brittle bones (osteoporosis).
● Do not use Tui Na on the hip area where an artificial joint is fitted.
● Avoid massaging directly on inflamed or broken skin, or over skin conditions such as eczema, psoriasis, or shingles. Treat people with these conditions elsewhere on the body.
● Do not massage the lower back or abdomen during pregnancy. In addition, some specific points should not be massaged during pregnancy. A Caution is given wherever these points are recommended in a treatment.

A Tui Na treatment

Tui Na is physically demanding for both the giver and the receiver. Both should wear comfortable, loose clothing to allow for easy movement. Cotton clothing is best, since synthetic fibres can affect the flow of Qi. The massage is given through clothing and the techniques do not use oils.

The room should be comfortable and warm. During the massage the receiver either sits on an upright chair or lies on a massage couch, depending on which part of the body is being treated. A strong table at hip height, padded with blankets, can be used instead of a massage couch, but a bed does not give firm enough support. Chapter Five explains preparing for treatment in more detail.

The receiver may find some of the Tui Na techniques uncomfortable initially, but they should never cause unbearable pain. After a vigorous kneading and pushing, the tissues and muscles will feel both pleasantly relaxed and invigorated.

Tui Na provides complete stimulation of the body's entire musculo-skeletal system, as well as all the internal organs. Since it rebalances Qi-flow the mind and the emotions will also be affected. In most cases a Tui Na treatment leaves the recipient feeling enlivened, happy, and sparkling with energy. However, in common with other forms of deep massage, Tui Na can sometimes release blocked emotional energy, with the effect that the receiver may feel "weepy" or emotional after the massage, or perhaps a day or two later. If this should happen, the Chinese way is to acknowledge these negative emotions, and then to let them go.

This book explains the Chinese view of health and the causes of disease, and shows you how to give a holistic whole-body Tui Na treatment to a partner, as well as techniques for treating common ailments and conditions. Chapter Two explains the theories of Traditional Chinese Medicine and how these differ from the Western medical approach. The 14 Meridians used in Tui Na are illustrated in Chapter Three, with clear descriptions to enable you to find the Qi-points – the points on the Meridians where Qi can most easily be manipulated.

Chapter Four concentrates on the basic techniques used in Tui Na massage. The chapter starts with soft tissue techniques: applying either static pressure or pressure with movement to the body tissues in order

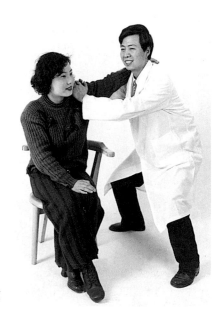

Dr Zhoa Shui-an of Xian College uses a joint manipulation to relieve "frozen shoulder".

to facilitate the smooth flow of Qi. These soft tissue techniques include pulling, pushing, squeezing, and kneading. The second part of this chapter deals with joint manipulation techniques which are similar to those used in osteopathy and chiropractic but give the added benefit of regulating Qi-flow. You will need to familiarize yourself with all the techniques so that you can apply them when they are used in the treatments in Chapters Five and Six.

The whole-body routine presented in Chapter Five provides step-by-step instructions for giving a Tui Na treatment to a partner. The routine starts with treatments on the neck and shoulders, and then works on the arms, back, legs, and feet, ending with Tui Na on the trunk and head.

One of the strengths of Tui Na is its application to sports' injuries of the muscles and joints. Some of these techniques are described in Chapter Six. This chapter also presents treatments for some common ailments and conditions, and Tui Na that is particularly suitable for infants, adolescents, and the elderly. Although some of the main benefits of Tui Na come from the interaction of Qi between the giver and receiver, there are some techniques that you can use effectively on yourself. These are described in a self-massage routine which, used daily, will increase your energy levels, boost your immune system, and promote health and wellbeing, leaving you sparkling all day.

Chapter Two

Traditional Chinese Medicine

To understand the healing power of Tui Na it is important to understand how Chinese medical theory views the causes of disease.

Disease does not suddenly occur. On the journey from health into disease a variety of symptoms will appear over a period of time, such as tiredness, pains in specific areas, insomnia, nausea, and dizziness. The onset of disease may manifest physically, emotionally, mentally, or even spiritually. To the Chinese doctor such symptoms indicate an imbalance in the flow of Qi. Patterns in the patient's physical and emotional states, in their behaviour, and in their living environment, will indicate the type of imbalance and the treatment required.

Western medicine tends to look for an agent causing an ailment, such as a virus or bacterium. Where the cause of a disease is not clear, it concentrates on treating the symptoms. Thus Western medicine is rooted in the sciences of anatomy and physiology, which study the body as separate from the mind. In contrast, in Chinese medical theory body, mind, and spirit are seen as indivisible and interdependent, and treatment is usually designed to restore and maintain a state of health throughout, rather than cure only a diseased component. Thus a physical ailment is viewed as a reflection of disharmony in the whole being. To cure the ailment you must cure the root cause of this disharmony.

CHINESE VS WESTERN APPROACH

Lower back pain is a very common complaint, which many Western doctors will diagnose as sciatica, "wear and tear", or a slipped disc. Treatment is often with anti-inflammatory drugs and bed rest, with surgery as a final solution.

The Chinese doctor diagnoses the underlying energy imbalance causing the back pain. The Tui Na treatment would be massage on the Bladder and Gall Bladder Meridians of the back, and on specific points on these Meridians, together with joint manipulation of the lower back and hips.

Constant and eternal change

According to Chinese thinking, all life arises from the interaction of two complementary yet opposite forces: yin and yang. All phenomena in nature can be described in terms of these two opposites. They are in constant interaction: each has no existence on its own, but only in relation to the other. A good analogy is the relationship between day and night. To define night, you must have day; day changes into night and then night changes into day, in a continual process of transformation.

Everything in the universe can be described in terms of yin and yang, though nothing is completely one or the other. The yin-ness or yang-ness of any system defines the balance that exists at that instant in time between yin and yang. Even at its most yin, a system will always have a yang component. In other words, there is no absolute yin or yang, only the one relative to the other in a dynamic relationship. This being so, Chinese philosophy classifies pairs of opposite qualities as the yin-ish and yang-ish condition in each case. For example, yin corresponds to "soft", while its opposite quality, "hard", is more yang. Some more of these correspondences are shown in the table (above, right).

The yin–yang symbol at the beginning of this chapter illustrates the interdependence and interaction between the two complementary opposites. Yin is represented by the dark area, and yang by the light. The curve that divides them shows that yin and yang transform into each other, while the small circles illustrate how each contains the other.

Every aspect of the human body, mind, and spirit can be defined by the balance of yin and yang. For good health the balance between them must be maintained.

YIN	YANG
quiet	loud
shady	bright
feminine	masculine
midnight	midday
cold	hot
interior	exterior
lethargic	energetic
winter	summer

The Essential Substances

The Essential Substances of the body are Qi, Jing, Shen, Blood, and Body Fluids. Of these, Qi, Jing, and Shen are known as the Three Treasures (see page 16). Qi is the life force, the vital energy which is governed by the interaction of yin and yang. Qi permeates the universe and all living things. All life is the result of the dynamic interaction between Qi and matter; this interaction ends at death. In our bodies, Qi flows through channels called Meridians and supplies every Organ, the mind, and the spirit. Thus the way Qi flows in the body affects physical, mental, emotional, and spiritual wellbeing.

In health, Qi flows smoothly through the Meridians, and for this to happen yin and yang influences must be balanced. Every individual has an optimal distribution of Qi, through their personal yin–yang balance which gives the "sparkle" of health, energy, and vitality. If the flow of Qi is disturbed it may stagnate or become blocked, affecting the yin–yang balance, and disease will result.

The Chinese concept of Blood has a far wider meaning than "blood" in Western medicine. Blood is almost an extension of Qi because it originates in the heart and bone marrow as a product of the Qi provided by food and air. Blood nourishes the body by transporting food Qi, and moistening and lubricating the internal tissues and organs. Blood and Qi also support each other: Blood is produced by Qi and is moved by Qi. In turn, Qi is nourished by Blood.

All the other natural body liquids, such as sweat, saliva, mucus, tears, and joint fluid are classified as Body Fluids. Their function is to moisten the body tissues, muscles, organs, skin, and hair. The lighter, clearer fluids, such as sweat and tears are the *jin*, while the heavier, thicker fluids that lubricate the joints and provide cerebro-spinal fluid are called *ye*.

The Organs

In Traditional Chinese Medicine the Organs are seen not just as physical body parts, but in terms of their functions and their relationships with other parts of the body. There is some overlap with the Western physiological definition, but in general the Chinese definition of an Organ encompasses the related spiritual and emotional systems, as well as the physical. For example, in Western thinking the heart is a large muscle in the chest that pumps blood around the body. In the Chinese view the Heart functions are all the processes in the body that are controlled by Heart Qi. The Heart regulates the flow of Blood and also stores the spirit (Shen). When the Heart Qi and Blood are harmonious, the pulse is strong and the spirit is nourished. If Heart Qi is weak this may manifest in loss of memory, or insomnia – both symptoms of inharmonious Shen.

The principal Organs are called the Zang–Fu. The Zang are the solid, interior, more yin Organs: the Lungs, Pericardium, Heart, Spleen, Liver, and Kidney. The Fu

The Three Treasures

In Traditional Chinese Medicine, three fundamental forces are the energy behind every aspect of human existence. These Three Treasures are Qi, Jing, and Shen. Qi is the great activator, that makes things happen and keeps them happening in dynamic balance. It is the energy for all the life processes from conception to death and is also the body's protector, keeping the body warm and fighting off external pathogens. If Qi is deficient the body has less resistance to disease. We inherit Original Qi from our parents, and we acquire Qi from the food that we eat and the air that we breathe.

Jing is the carrier of the life force, the "mover" that determines the pattern of growth and development. High quality Jing creates a strong constitution. The actions of the Original Jing that we inherit from our parents are supplemented by Jing from food. Jing promotes the production of Kidney Qi, which is like a fountain from which all other forms of Qi flow, and also provides for the production of "marrow", which includes the brain and the spinal cord. Over-exertion can deplete Jing.

Shen is the Qi guide, the vitality behind Qi. It is the rarefied type of Qi that supports activity in the mind and spirit. Shen is associated with the personality and the power of the mind to form ideas: if it is not in harmony, muddled thinking and forgetfulness may result. We inherit Original Shen from our parents, and through our lives it is continually nourished from the air and food.

are the hollow, more external, yang Organs: the Stomach, Gall Bladder, Bladder, Large Intestine, Sanjiao, and Small Intestine. Each Zang Organ is paired with a Fu Organ. The principal functions of each of the Organs are described in Chapter Three.

For health the Organ systems must work together in harmony, sustaining the body activities. Qi is the energy that maintains the balance of yin and yang to support the Organ functions.

THE ZANG–FU

Zang Organs (YIN)	Fu Organs (YANG)
Lung	Large Intestine
Pericardium	Sanjiao
Heart	Small Intestine
Spleen	Stomach
Liver	Gall Bladder
Kidney	Bladder

These lucky talisman figures represent longevity, wisdom, and prosperity – which in the Chinese view result from a healthy, well balanced life.

SANJIAO AND PERICARDIUM

The Sanjiao has no equivalent in Western anatomy. In Chinese medicine its function is to regulate the circulation and exchange of Body Fluids. It is sometimes called the Triple Warmer or Triple Burner.

The Pericardium is sometimes called the Heart Protector. It is usually regarded by the Chinese as part of the Heart and not as an Organ in its own right.

The Meridians

The Chinese recognize that it is not only the absolute level of Qi in the body that is significant in the maintenance of health, but the way it is distributed and balanced throughout the body. Every one of the billions of cells that make up the human body needs to be suffused constantly with Qi to enable it to function normally. The Meridian system is the network that distributes Qi around the body, linking all the parts of the body, mind, and spirit, and the Essential Substances.

The Meridians are not physical channels, in the way that veins and arteries are channels for blood. They cannot be examined by dissection. The system of Meridians has been well documented in Chinese medicine over the past four thousand years, and recently has been confirmed by scientific experiments which show that the Meridians have a different electric potential from the surrounding tissues. Using instruments that measure very small electrical currents, the precise routes of these energetic pathways and their Qi-points have been traced, and found to correspond to those on ancient Chinese Meridian charts.

Each Meridian controls Qi associated with one of the principal internal Organs, after which it is named. There are twelve Meridians in each half of the body, and they occur symmetrically. Six of the Meridians are yang. Of these, the Stomach, Gall Bladder, and Bladder Meridians start on the head and end on the toes, while the Large Intestine, Sanjiao, and Small Intestine Meridians start at the fingertips and end on the head. The other six Meridians are yin. The Spleen, Liver, and Kidney Meridians start in the toes and end in the chest region, while the Lung, Pericardium, and Heart Meridians start in the chest and end on the fingers.

The Ren and Du Meridians encircle the body on the midline. The Ren Meridian is yin and the Du is yang.

In common with acupuncture, Tui Na works on these twelve Meridians and the Ren and Du. Along each Meridian there are specific areas, called Qi-points, where Qi flows near to the body surface. Here Qi-flow can be manipulated, either by using needles, as in acupuncture, or using deep pressure in Tui Na massage. These treatments can clear blockages and stagnant Qi, enabling the Qi to flow freely and balancing yin and yang.

The paths of the Meridians and the exact positions of the Qi-points are described and illustrated in Chapter Three.

FINDING QI-POINTS

Qi-points often feel tender to the touch, and it is this tenderness that tells you when you have found the right place. To feel this sensation, find the Qi-points near the beginning of the Bladder Meridian known as Bladder 2 (**BL 2**), which are on the innermost edges of the eyebrows. Using the middle fingers of both hands, press firmly on the inside tip of your eyebrows. Make small circular movements until you feel a slight indentation and a tender sensation different from the sensation from pressing around the point.

When you have found the points, knead them deeply with your middle fingers for about one minute. These **BL 2** points are effective in treating sore eyes and headaches on the front of the head.

THE SIX MERIDIANS OF THE HAND
*These yin Meridians start on the chest
and end on the fingers*
Lung
Pericardium
Heart

*These yang Meridians start on the fingers
and end on the chest*
Large Intestine
Sanjiao
Small Intestine

THE SIX MERIDIANS OF THE FOOT
*These yin Meridians start on the feet
and end on the chest*
Spleen
Liver
Kidney

*These yang Meridians start on the head
and end on the feet*
Stomach
Gall Bladder
Bladder

CASE STUDY

Mark was 51 years old when he first came for Tui Na treatment and had always suffered from back trouble. He had undergone an operation on his back some 20 years previously to remove a damaged lumbar disc. As a result, movement in this region was limited. He had stiffness in his upper back and pain at the base of his spine. He suffered constant pain in his neck and shoulders and severe "tennis elbow". Unable to lead the life he wanted, he was stressed and miserable.

Mark had tried other therapies – osteopathy, chiropractic, physiotherapy – but nothing seemed to have any real effect. He describes finding Tui Na as discovering "a little gem". After the first treatment Mark's back felt very tender from the deep, vigorous work the therapist had done on his body, but he also felt energized and full of wellbeing. "I felt like I was walking on air." Two days later his shoulders and lower back felt loose and relaxed and his elbow pain was much reduced. Four years on, Mark has Tui Na treatment every fortnight to keep the pain at bay and has never needed to return to his doctor. He has achieved and maintained positive good health.

Regular Tui Na keeps Qi-flow balanced and so is preventative, keeping problems from developing in the first place. Having a healthy body also contributes to a healthy mind. Mark says, "Those who are lucky enough to experience Tui Na will be aware of its incredible ability to de-stress the body, and to soothe and calm the mind. I am far more relaxed now and able to cope with stress. I have experienced the feel-good factor."

The Five Elements

Chinese philosophy identifies five different ways that Qi manifests itself in the universe as the Five Elements: Fire, Water, Earth, Wood, and Metal. As part of the universe, the human body and mind is also subject to the energies of these Elements. Each Zang–Fu Organ pair and its associated Meridians is dominated by one of the Five Elemental energies. Any imbalances in the energies of one Element will show up as symptoms in one or both of the Organs in the pair and in their Meridians.

The simplest disturbance of Qi-flow occurs within the energies of one Element. For example, an imbalance in the Wood Element can affect the Liver Organ and Meridian, or the Gall Bladder Organ and Meridian, or both. The associations between the Organs, their Meridians, and the Elements are shown in the outer ring of the diagram on the facing page. Each Element (in the centre of the diagram) dominates one Organ pair (on the outer ring), with the exception of Fire, which influences two pairs: the Heart and Small Intestine, plus two "extras", the Pericardium and Sanjiao.

The diagram also shows the relationship between the Elements and other "correspondences". Each Element has a related emotion, and also a specific body part. For example, bones are related to Water, and bone problems such as osteoarthritis could reflect an imbalance in the Water Element.

It is the same for the outlet in the body. The ear is the outlet related to Water and any imbalance of Water energies could affect the sense of hearing. Each Element is also associated with a particular colour, a season, a type of weather, and a taste, all of which are shown in the diagram. Chinese medicine pays great attention to a patient's coloration, and also their smell, from which a doctor can detect imbalance in an Element.

This network of Element associations reflects the complex ways that we interact with our environment and provides a way of describing and explaining the effects of this interaction. A knowledge of the Five Element theory assists a Chinese medical practitioner in interpreting a patient's emotional and physical reactions to external factors and making a diagnosis.

The Five Elements also interact with each other in the same way that they do in nature. Wood produces Fire (as fuel), Fire produces Earth (as Ashes), Earth produces Metal (as ore), Metal produces Water (melting when heated), and Water produces Wood (by feeding trees). This cycle is indicated by the clockwise arrows in the centre of the diagram on the facing page. In the same way the Organs corresponding to the Five Elements are linked in a creative cycle, with each Element passing energy on to the next. In this way the Liver (Wood) sustains and supports the Heart (Fire), which in turn supports the Stomach. An untreated problem in the Organs associated with Wood, for example, could lead to imbalance in Fire, resulting in forgetfulness or palpitations. However, if the Wood Element energies are relatively too strong, the Fire burns out of control and affects the Earth Element.

There is also a control cycle, shown by the second set of arrows in the centre of the diagram, which similarly reflects interactions in nature. For example, Fire controls Metal by melting it. In the body, a heart condition caused by excessive Fire can affect the lungs, leading to breathlessness, a symptom of imbalance of Metal energies.

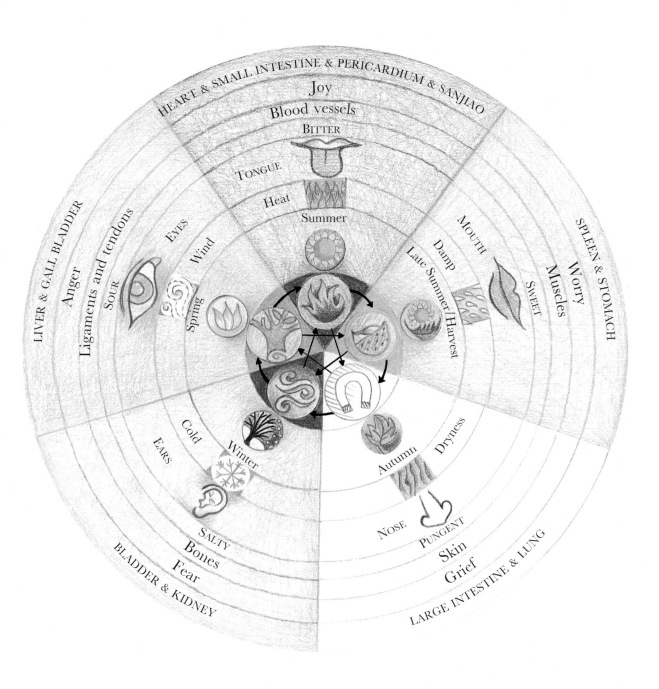

The central symbols represent the Five Elements.
Starting at the top and following the clockwise arrows
they are: Fire, Earth, Metal, Water, and Wood.

Chapter Three

Meridians and Qi-points

The classical system of Meridians was first mapped over 4000 years ago and is the basis of all Traditional Chinese Medicine. On these Meridians there are approximately 365 Qi-points, where Qi-flow can be manipulated to restore balance and harmony. Massage at each of the Qi-points has slightly different effects on Qi, and each Qi-point has a defined therapeutic function. Tui Na is thus a very precise therapy. The practitioner builds up a picture of the patient's pattern of disharmony (see page 14), and from this and knowledge of the Meridians and their specific Qi-points, decides which treatments to give.

Most Qi-points can be used to treat problems in their immediate vicinity. These are local points. Many also have healing potential for conditions that are distant from the points themselves, and these are called distant points. An example is **LI 4** on the hand, which treats headaches. This ability of Qi-points to affect distant parts of the body gives Tui Na the power to treat all kinds of problems in places where your hands cannot reach. In particular, distant points can be used where there is eczema, bruising, or other skin conditions in the local area.

Massaging along a Meridian ensures that all blockages of Qi in that Meridian are cleared, improving Qi-flow along it. Parts of the whole-body routine in Chapter Five involve working along a Meridian, so it is important to be familiar with the Meridian pathways in the body. Knowledge of the Meridians also enables you to use distant points in treatments. Pages 26–51 show each Meridian, along with the Qi-points used.

The Qi-points are all numbered, and named after the Meridians on which they are found, for example Gall Bladder 20, or Large Intestine 4. The standard abbreviations for these are given in the table, far right. There are approximately 100 Qi-points that are particularly powerful and effective in Tui Na, and that are most useful for treating common ailments and symptoms. These points, given in the chart on page 25, are used in the treatments in Chapters Five and Six.

Finding Qi-points

The positions of the Qi-points are given with reference to body landmarks, such as a bone or muscle. The illustrations on pages 138–9 in the Appendix show the bones and muscles used in the Qi-point descriptions in this chapter. Measurements from these landmarks are given in *cun* (pronounced "soon"), which is also called an Anatomical Chinese Inch or ACI. A *cun* is not a standard measurement: it varies from person to person, and changes as we grow from child to adult. Your personal *cun* is the width of the top of your thumb. There are a fixed number of *cun* between body landmarks: for example, the distance from the outer kneecap to the ankle is 16 *cun*, while the distance from elbow crease to wrist crease is 12 *cun*. Techniques for measuring in *cun* are explained more fully on page 138 in the Appendix.

The Meridian illustrations on pages 28–51 show the Qi-points and describe their positions using this system of "landmarks" and *cun*. Practise finding some Qi-points, both on yourself and your partner, so that you are familiar with the measuring technique before you start on the whole-body routine in Chapter Five. Qi-points generally feel tender when pressed, even when the Qi-flow is in balance, so you will know when you have found the correct point.

A Qi-point that feels particularly tender may indicate an underlying energy problem which needs pressure treatment to balance Qi-flow. For example, people with joint or muscle pain are often unable to pinpoint the exact site of the pain. During a Tui Na treatment of Qi-points in the area, they may realize that the pain is centred on one of these points. Deep massage on such points often brings speedy pain relief.

MERIDIAN ABBREVIATIONS

Liver	**LV**
Gall Bladder	**GB**
Heart	**H**
Small Intestine	**SI**
Pericardium	**P**
Sanjiao	**SJ**
Spleen	**SP**
Stomach	**ST**
Lung	**LU**
Large Intestine	**LI**
Kidney	**K**
Bladder	**BL**
Ren	**R**
Du	**D**

Special Qi-points

In addition to the specific therapeutic local functions, some Qi-points have energy links with other Meridians or Organ systems. The *Shu* points, on the Bladder Meridian on the back, are each related to a specific Organ, and are named after the Organ they affect: Heart Point, Spleen Point, and so on. There are also Influential points for the Bones and Blood. Massage on a *Shu* point has a very strong effect on the related Organ. For example, treating the Kidney point **BL 23** has a powerful effect on Kidney Qi.

A massage covering all the *Shu* points stimulates all the body's systems, boosting and balancing Qi-flow. For a quick and effective preventative treatment to maintain good health, work through all these points, as described in the back massage section, in Part Three of the whole-body routine in Chapter Five.

Tui Na also identifies certain points that are particularly valuable in stimulating and strengthening the immune system to help the body resist infection. Regular treatment of these Health Care points balances the Organ functions, reduces the effects of stress, and stimulates Qi-flow. The whole-body routine works on all these points, but for general good health you can give yourself a daily workout, kneading all the Health Care points listed below. The positions of all these points are shown and described on the Meridian illustrations on pages 28–51.

SHU POINTS

Lung Point	**BL 13**
Pericardium Point	**BL 14**
Heart Point	**BL 15**
Liver Point	**BL 18**
Gall Bladder Point	**BL 19**
Spleen Point	**BL 20**
Stomach Point	**BL 21**
Sanjiao Point	**BL 22**
Kidney Point	**BL 23**
Large Intestine Point	**BL 25**
Bladder Point	**BL 28**

INFLUENTIAL POINTS

Blood	**BL 17**
Bone	**BL 11**

HEALTH CARE POINTS

GB 20, GB 21, GB 30
ST 36
LI 4 Caution: do not use **LI 4** during pregnancy.
LI 10, LI 11, LI 20
LU 7
P 6
H 7
K 1, K 3
SP 6 Caution: do not use **SP 6** during pregnancy.
LV 3
BL 2, BL 23
R 6
D 20
Yintang
Taiyang

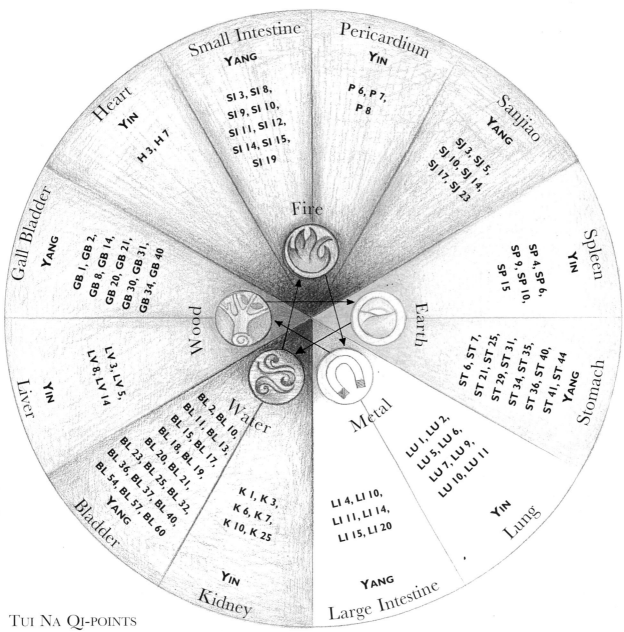

TUI NA QI-POINTS

These Qi-points are the ones that Maria Mercati has found are the most effective in treating chronic and acute conditions with Tui Na. In the chart they are grouped according to their relationships with the Organs and the Five Elements.

The Meridians are each associated with an Organ, and are named after that Organ. They are also paired, in the same way as the yin Organs are paired with yang Organs in the Zang–Fu (see page 17). Thus the Liver Meridian is paired with the Gall Bladder Meridian; the Stomach with the Spleen, and so on. Each Meridian meets its paired Meridian at one of its ends: for example, the Liver Meridian joins the Gall Bladder Meridian in the foot.

The twelve paired Meridians each occur symmetrically on either side of the body. Where a Qi-point is recommended for treatment you should treat that point on both sides of the body. However, when treating a local pain or injury, only use the local points on the side affected. The two unpaired Meridians, the Ren and Du occur singly, since they run along the midline of the body.

Each Meridian pair is dominated by the energies of one of the Five Elements (see page 20) and the pages that follow present the Meridians according to their ruling Element. Each describes the functions of the Meridians and Organs associated with that Element, and possible effects of an imbalance in that Element. A case study shows how a Tui Na practitioner would diagnose and treat such imbalances in the Element energies. These pages are coded using the colours associated with the Elements: red for Fire, green for Wood, and so on. Illustrations of the Meridians associated with that Element show all the Qi-points used in the treatments in Chapters Five and Six.

For clarity the Qi-points are illustrated on only one side of the body and each point is labelled on the illustration. Captions give the Chinese names (see right), clear instructions for finding the point, and a list of the specific effects of treatment on that point.

CHINESE NAMES

The Chinese name of a Qi-point often reflects either the position or the function of the point.

LI 20 is YINXIANG, translated as Welcome Fragrance or Meeting of a Good Smell. Found in the depression on the outside of the nostril, this is the last point of the Large Intestine Meridian. Massage on **LI 20** helps the Lung to perform its dispersing function, clearing a blocked nose and enabling it to smell fragrant scents again – hence the name Welcome Fragrance.

LU 10 is YUJI, or Fish Belly. The point is at the base of the thumb, where the skin changes colour and type. The name describes the appearance of the large muscle at the base of the thumb.

BL 60 is KUNLUN, which means Big and High, and is also the name of a famous Chinese Mountain. The point is beside the outside ankle bone and its name serves as a reminder that it is next to a prominent feature.

BL 10 is TIANZHU, translated as Celestial Pillar or Column of Heaven. The point is on the neck: the pillar that supports the head.

BL 1 is JINGMENG, which means Eye Brightness. This point at the inner corner of the eye is used for treating eye disorders, thus brightening the eyes.

The Wood Element

The Liver is the yin Organ influenced by the energies of the Wood element. It is paired with the yang Gall Bladder Organ.

CASE STUDY

Paul is 35 years old and suffers from severe migraine headaches. The pain tends to settle over his right eye, giving him slightly blurred vision and he also feels pain at the base of his skull and at the top of his right shoulder.

He is easily irritated both with his wife and with colleagues at work. His job entails taking business dinners, where he tends to drink to excess. Paul works out at the gym once a week, and injured his lower back a month ago. Since then he has had pains down his right leg, which stop him sleeping, thus making his headache worse. His doctor has prescribed anti-inflammatory drugs and tranquillizers.

Paul's symptoms all indicate an imbalance in the Wood energies. He is quick to anger, the emotion under the control of the Liver Organ. The Liver also influences all the body's muscles and tendons, which are causing him pain. The sites of his aches and pains show that work is needed on the Gall Bladder Meridian, which will give access to Liver Qi, and also on specific points on the Liver Meridian. Treatment on the Liver and Gall Bladder *Shu* points (see page 24) will also be beneficial. Paul should also try to reduce his alcohol consumption.

THE LIVER ORGAN
- moves Qi through the body
- stimulates physical movement, mental and emotional activity
- stores Blood
- affects tendons and ligaments
- governs nail health
- opens into the eyes
- is related to anger

THE GALL BLADDER ORGAN
- stores bile
- affects tendons

THE LIVER MERIDIAN
Treatment on Liver Meridian Qi-points is recommended for:
- headaches, dizziness, and facial spasm
- PMT that includes lower abdominal pain
- anger

THE GALL BLADDER MERIDIAN
Treatment on Gall Bladder Meridian Qi-points is recommended for:
- migraine
- ear problems
- liver problems
- pain in the muscles around the ribs
- pain in the neck, shoulder, side of leg, knee, and outer ankle
- sciatica

Liver Meridian

LV 1 is on the inner margin of the big toe just behind the nail, and the Meridian ends at **LV 14**, between the 6th and 7th ribs directly below the nipple.

CASE STUDY

Robert is 25 years old and a keen rugby player. He is having an enforced lay-off from the game due to an injury to a hamstring tendon on the inside of his left knee. Since the injury happened some four weeks ago, he has been feeling frustrated and easily irritated. He has also complained of headaches.

These symptoms indicate an imbalance in the Liver energies. The recommended treatment is deep kneading of **LV 8** to treat the knee problem and of **LV 3** to treat irritability and frustration. In a full Tui Na session, other Meridians would also be treated in conjunction with these.

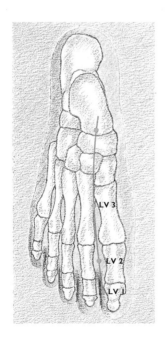

LV 14 QIMEN

On the chest directly below the nipple in the space between the 6th and 7th ribs. Treats vomiting, pain in the upper abdomen.

LV 8 QUQUAN

Just above the inner end of the crease behind the knee when the knee is flexed. Treats knee problems.

LV 5 LIGOU

5 cun above the inner ankle bone, just off the edge of the tibia. Treats impotence in men and excess libido; also important for male and female external genitals.

LV 3 TAICHONG

In a depression just in front of the point where the first and second metatarsal bones come together. Calms emotional problems, especially anger; treats headaches and migraine, liver problems such as sclerosis and hepatitis, gall bladder problems, and irregular menstruation.

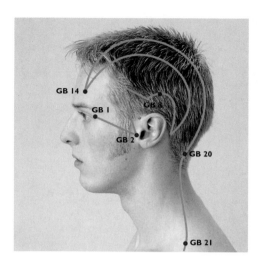

Gall Bladder Meridian

This Meridian starts at **GB 1**, in a small depression just beyond the outer corner of the eye, and ends at **GB 44** on the outer margin of the 4th toe just behind the nail.

GB 1 TONGZILIAO
In a small depression just beyond the outer corner of the eye. Treats eye problems, pain in the brow ridges.

GB 2 TINGHUI
In a depression felt when the mouth is open, just in front of the ear and level with the notch above the ear lobe. Treats ear problems such as tinnitus, poor hearing.

GB 8 SHUAIGU
1.5 cun directly above the top of the ear. Treats migraine headaches.

GB 14 YANGBAI
1 cun above the midpoint of the eyebrow. Treats facial paralysis, frontal headache, twitching eyelids.

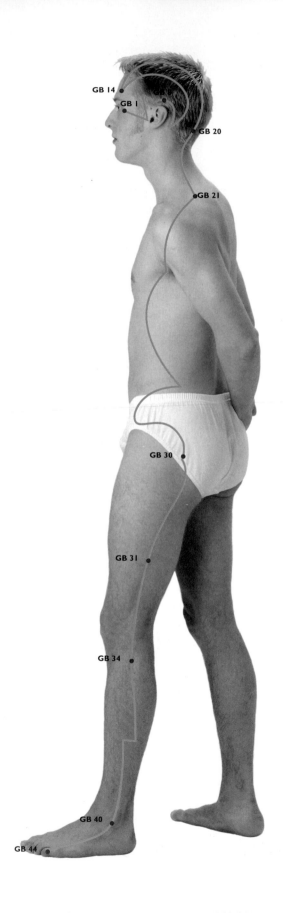

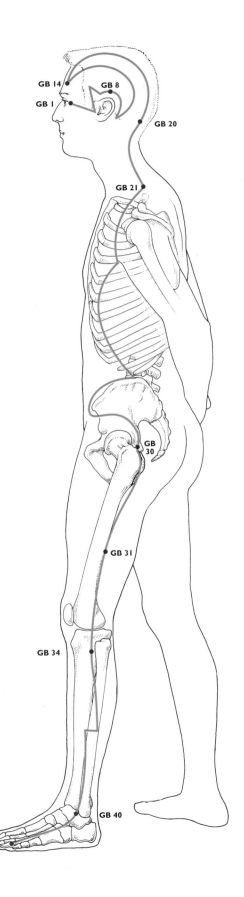

GB 20 FENGCHI

At the top of the nape of the neck, in the large depression immediately below the base of the skull. Treats all kinds of headache, even those resulting from a blow; problems affecting eyes, ears, and nose, tension of neck muscles, cervical spondylitis, flu and common cold, Parkinson's syndrome, epilepsy, and facial paralysis.

GB 21 JIANJING

In the middle of a line drawn from the spinous process of cervical vertebra 7 to the back corner of the shoulder joint (acromion). Treats neck pain and stiffness, pain in the shoulder.

GB 30 HUANTIAO

One-third of the way along a line from the outer edge of the hip bone to the coccyx. Treats lumbago, sciatica, pain in the hip region, weakness in the lower leg, heel pain.

GB 31 FENGSHI

Just where the tip of the middle finger touches the side of the thigh when standing with arms relaxed at the side. Treats numbness of the thigh region, sciatica.

GB 34 YANGLINGQUAN

In the depression just in front of and slightly below the head of the fibula. Treats muscle spasm and cramp in the lower leg, weakness and paralysis of the lower leg, knee and ankle pain including acute pain resulting from sprain; sciatica, stiff neck, and pain in the rib muscles. Has a powerfully relaxing effect on muscles in general.

GB 40 QIUXU

At the lower front edge of the outer ankle bone. Treats pain in the muscles of the rib cage, ankle sprain if not accompanied by significant swelling. Helps to relax muscles throughout the body.

The Fire Element

The Heart and Pericardium are the yin
Organs influenced by the energies of the
Fire Element. Their paired yang Organs are
the Small Intestine and Sanjiao Organs,
respectively.

CASE STUDY

Since Alan's wife died from cancer two years ago
he has been taking tranquillizers for depression.
He still feels very lonely, empty, and broken-
hearted. His face is pale and he lacks all sparkle.
Alan sheds tears as he talks of his wife. He also
complains of pain between his shoulder blades.

Alan's symptoms indicate an imbalance in the
Fire Element, which governs the Heart and Small
Intestine. The Heart houses the mind and spirit,
and strengthening its function will help relieve
Alan's emotional pain. His shoulder pain suggests
that the Small Intestine and Sanjiao Meridians
should be treated to gain access to Heart Qi. Alan
should have treatment on the arms, shoulders,
and mid-upper back, and also on the Heart Point,
BL 15 (see *Shu* points, page 24).

THE HEART ORGAN
- controls the transformation of food Qi into Blood
- powers the circulation of Blood
- maintains the condition of the blood vessels
- houses the mind and the Shen (see page 16)
- manifests in the face
- opens into the tongue
- is related to joy

THE SMALL INTESTINE ORGAN
- affects partially digested food
- affects Body Fluids

THE PERICARDIUM ORGAN
- has a similar function to the Heart
- can reduce vomiting and nausea

THE SANJIAO ORGAN
- regulates the Body Fluids

THE HEART MERIDIAN
Treatment on Heart Meridian Qi-points is recommended for:
- heart problems: cardiac pain, palpitations
- depression, insomnia
- wrist pain, golfer's elbow
- tongue problems

THE SMALL INTESTINE MERIDIAN
*Treatment on Small Intestine Meridian Qi-points
is recommended for:*
- pain in the shoulder blade, mid-upper back,
and neck
- pain in the wrist and elbow

THE PERICARDIUM MERIDIAN
*Treatment on Pericardium Meridian Qi-points
is recommended for:*
- heart and chest problems
- heartbreak and anxiety, panic attacks
- carpal tunnel syndrome

THE SANJIAO MERIDIAN
*Treatment on Sanjiao Meridian Qi-points
is recommended for:*
- ear and eye problems
- migraine
- pain in the ribs
- problems in the side of the neck
- pain in the shoulder joint, wrist, and elbow

Heart Meridian

H 1 is in the centre of the armpit, and the
Heart Meridian ends at **H 9**, at the base of the
little finger nail on the inside edge.

H 3 SHAOHAI

*At the extreme inner end of the crease
formed when the arm is bent at the elbow.*
Treats local pain in the elbow, and
atrophied muscles of the arm lying
on the Heart Meridian.

H 7 SHENMEN

*On the underside of the wrist, in line with
the little finger. It is in a depression on the
main wrist crease.* Treats restless
mind, insomnia, shallow sleep,
depression, heart pain
and palpitations, tongue
problems such as
ulceration and soreness.

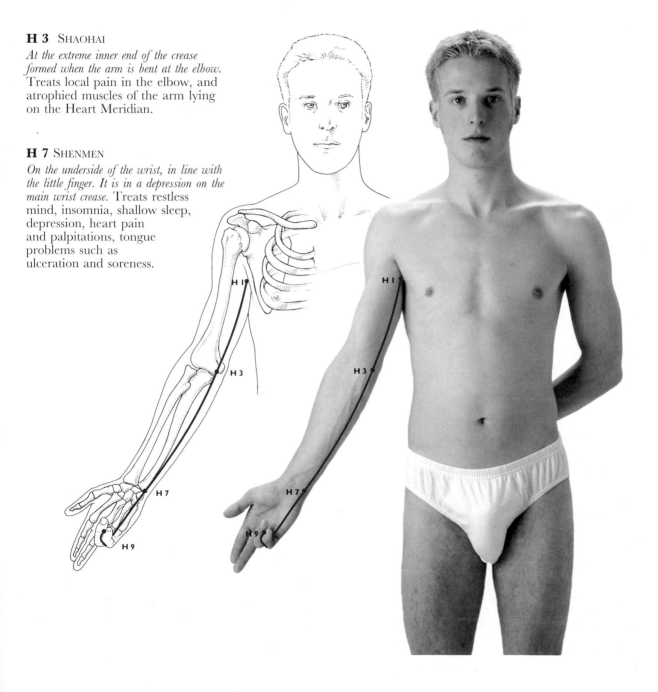

Small Intestine Meridian

This Meridian starts at **SI 1** on the outer edge of the little finger just behind the nail, and ends on **SI 19** in front of the ear opening.

SI 19 TIANGGONG
In front of the ear opening in a depression felt when the mouth is open. Treats ear problems.

SI 15 JIANZHONSHU
2 cun from the midline, level with the lower border of cervical vertebra 7. Treats neck stiffness, shoulder and back pain.

SI 14 JIANWAISHU
Just off the upper inside angle of the scapula, 3 cun from the midline level with the lower margin of the spinous process of thoracic vertebra 1. Treats shoulder pain, neck stiffness, pain between the shoulder blades.

SI 12 BINGFENG
*Vertically up from **SI 11** just over the scapular spine.* Treats shoulder pain.

SI 11 TIANZONG
In a depression approximately in the centre of the scapula. Treats the same conditions as **SI 10**, plus pain between the shoulder blades.

SI 10 NAOSHU
*Vertically above **SI 9** just inside and below the outer end of the shoulder bone.* Treats pain and injury in shoulders, arm paralysis, numbness and pain anywhere along the Small Intestine Meridian.

SI 9 JIANZHEN
1 cun above the end of the crease behind the armpit when the arm is held close to the body. Treats arm immobility and shoulder pain.

SI 8 XIAOHAI
In the groove beneath the elbow between the lower end of the humerus and the top of the ulna. Treats arm numbness or pain.

SI 3 HOUXI
On the outer end of the main crease formed by the knuckles of the clenched fist. Treats pain on the outside of the hand and arm, little finger numbness, and neck stiffness.

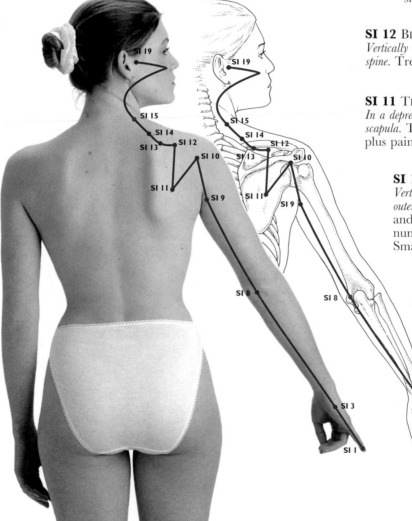

Pericardium Meridian

P 1 is on the chest just beside the nipple in
the space between the 4th and 5th ribs.
The Meridian ends at **P 9** on the centre
of the tip of the middle finger.

P 6 NEIGUAN
*On the underside of the forearm, 2 cun above the middle crease
on the wrist, almost exactly in the midline between the two
large tendons.* Treats nausea and sickness, especially
travel sickness, emotional pain resulting from affairs
of the heart, insomnia, erratic heartbeat, calms restlessness. This point ranks with **LI 4** and **ST 36** as
one of the most powerful. Regular stimulation for
several minutes helps to strengthen the Heart.
Caution: do not use **LI 4** during pregnancy.

P 7 DALING
*In the middle of the underside of the wrist on
the middle wrist crease.* Treats anxiety
and palpitations, carpal tunnel
syndrome, wrist pain, numbness of
thumb, index, and middle fingers.

P 8 LAOGONG
*Where the nail touches the palm when the
middle finger is flexed.* Treats a restless
and disturbed mind, cardiac pain.

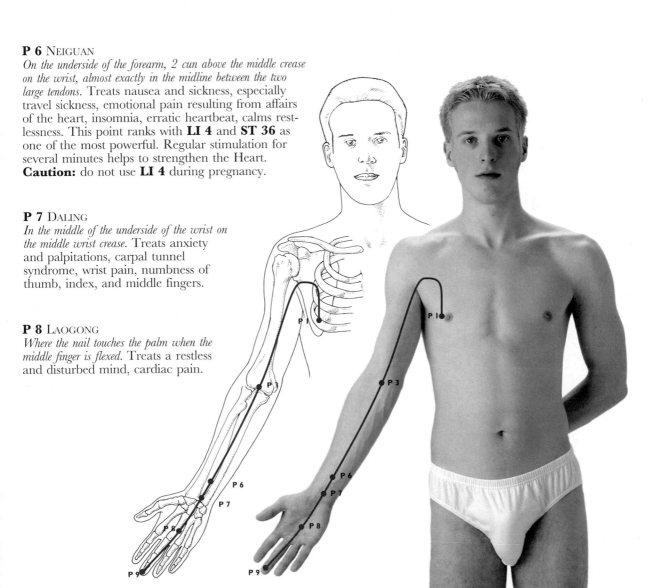

Sanjiao Meridian

The Meridian starts at **SJ 1,** on the outside of the
4th finger just behind the nail and ends at **SJ 23** on
the outside tip of the eyebrow.

SJ 3 ZHONGZHU
*At the top of the depression between the 4th and 5th
metacarpal bones just behind the knuckles.* Treats ear
problems, poor hearing, migraine where the pain is
on the side of the head, pain, stiffness, or swelling in
the back of the hand.

SJ 5 WAIGUAN
*On the opposite side of the forearm to **P 6**, 2 cun up from
the main crease on the back of the wrist between the radius
and the ulna.* Treats shoulder pain, numbness in the
4th finger, lateral headaches, hearing problems,
fever caused by colds.

SJ 10 TIANJING
*In the depression approximately 1 cun above base of the
humerus when elbow is flexed.* Treats elbow pain.

SJ 14 JIANLIAO
*In a depression just below the outer tip of the
acromion (back of shoulder joint).* Treats
shoulder pain and immobility.

SJ 17 YIFENG
*Behind the ear in the centre of the
depression just behind the lobe.* Treats
ear problems such as tinnitus and
deafness, facial paralysis, toothache
and neuralgia in the lower jaw.

SJ 23 SIZHUKONG
*In a small depression at the outer tip
of the eyebrow.* Treats headaches
on the side of the head,
dizziness, facial paralysis,
muscle twitching in or
near the eyelids, and
conjunctivitis.

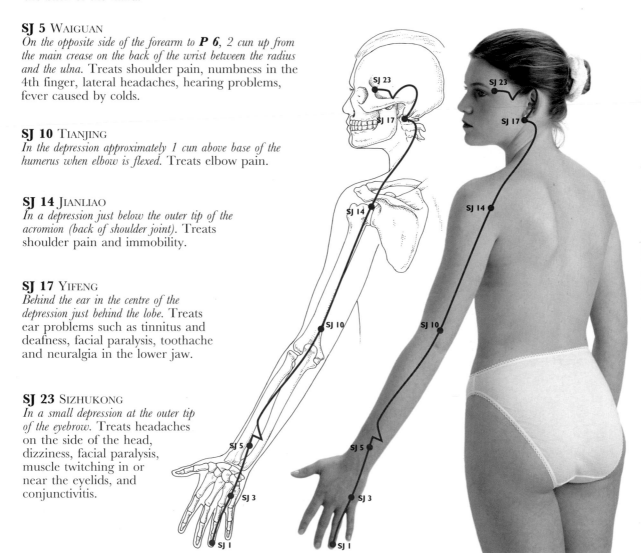

The Earth Element

The Spleen is the yin Organ influenced by the energies of the Earth Element. Its paired yang Organ is the Stomach.

CASE STUDY

Mary is a successful training consultant whose husband has recently left her for another woman. She suffers from insomnia, spending much of her sleeping as well as waking time analysing the possible reasons for her situation. This causes her extreme emotional pain and worry, which in turn makes her overeat for comfort. Her stomach feels bloated, tight, and uncomfortable. Mary's GP says she possibly has irritable bowel syndrome. Mary also complains of tense neck and shoulder muscles and a feeling of general heaviness.

Mary's symptoms indicate an imbalance in the Earth energies of the Spleen and Stomach. The Spleen controls the emotion worry, and the Stomach and Spleen Qi-points in the abdomen will give access to the Spleen Qi. Mary also needs general massage, which will boost her vitality and wellbeing, helping her to relax and to feel better about herself and her ability to cope. The treatment should also focus on the neck, shoulders, and abdomen, and the Bladder Meridian *Shu* points for Spleen and Stomach, **BL 20** and **BL 21** (see page 24).

THE SPLEEN ORGAN

- extracts Qi from food absorbed by the Stomach
- stabilizes the circulation of blood within the blood vessels
- opens into the mouth cavity
- governs the body's central Qi
- controls the flow of refined Qi into the extremities
- is related to worry

THE STOMACH ORGAN

- separates pure essence from food
- sends impure essence to the Small Intestine for further processing
- dispatches pure essence to the Spleen

THE SPLEEN MERIDIAN

Treatment on Spleen Meridian Qi-points is recommended for:
- spleen and stomach problems
- abdominal bloating
- oedema in the legs and ankles
- PMT and menstrual problems
- bruising
- insomnia
- worry

THE STOMACH MERIDIAN

Treatment on Stomach Meridian Qi-points is recommended for:
- head and face problems: headache, toothache, jawache, facial paralysis
- abdominal bloating, diarrhoea, and constipation
- pain in the knee and front of leg
- boosting the immune system

Spleen Meridian

The Spleen Meridian starts at **SP 1,** on the outer margin of the big toe just behind the nail and ends at **SP 21,** 6 *cun* below the armpit between the 6th and 7th ribs.

CASE STUDY

Sophie is eighteen years old and a student. In two months' time she has some important examinations, which she needs to pass well in order to gain a university place to study dentistry. Although she is hard working and very intelligent, Sophie is very anxious that she will not achieve the grades she needs, and she is not sleeping well. Also, in the week before her menstrual period she feels heavy and uncomfortable, and her abdomen becomes very bloated.

Sophie's symptoms indicate an imbalance of the Spleen energies. Daily treatment on **SP 4** and **SP 6** for at least one week will help to relieve her pre-menstrual symptoms and her anxiety. In a full Tui Na session, other Meridians would also be treated in conjunction with these. **Caution:** do not use **SP 6** during pregnancy.

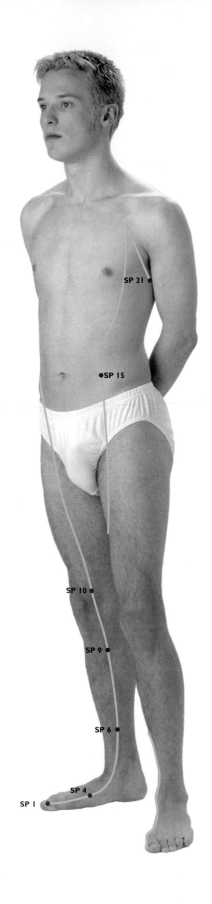

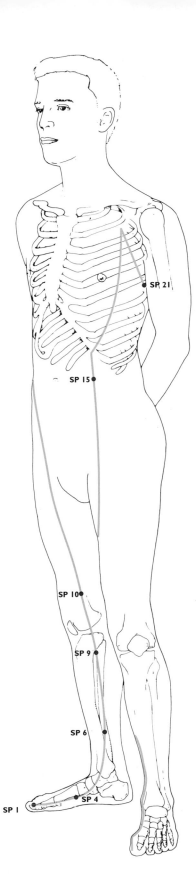

SP 15 DAHENG
On the abdomen level with and 4 cun to the side of the navel. Improves bowel rhythm.

SP 10 XUEHAI
2 cun above the top edge of the kneecap on a vertical line drawn along the inner border of the patella and up the thigh. Treats itchiness of the skin, eczema, psoriasis and urticaria (hives), irregularities in the menstrual cycle.

SP 9 YINLINGQUAN
In a depression between the tibia and the calf muscle, found by rubbing a finger up the inside edge of the tibia until the angle of the bone surface changes. Treats gastric pain, oedema, and diarrhoea.

SP 6 SANYINJIAO
Under the inside edge of the tibia, 3 cun above the tip of the inner ankle bone. Treats diarrhoea and abdominal swelling, bleeding, hernia and prolapse, insomnia and restless sleep, difficult labour, irregularities in the menstrual cycle, impotence and premature ejaculation, difficulty in passing urine.
Caution: do not use this point during pregnancy.

SP 4 KUNGSUN
In the middle of the arch of the foot, just beneath the upper end of the first metatarsal. Treats depression, abdominal pain, insomnia.

Stomach Meridian

The Stomach Meridian starts at **ST 1,** just above the lower edge of the eye socket in line with the pupil, and ends at **ST 45** on the outside of the second toe, just behind the nail.

ST 6 JIACHE
In the middle of the mass of jaw muscle just above and in front of the angle of the lower jaw bone where the muscle is most prominent. Treats toothache in the lower jaw, and facial paralysis.

ST 7 XIAGUAN
*Directly above **ST 6** in the notch between the jawbone and cheek bone; easy to find if the mouth is opened and closed.* Treats poor hearing, upper jaw toothache, and facial paralysis. Deep pressure on this point has a strong painkilling effect for dental treatment.

ST 21 LIANGMEN
4 cun above the centre of the navel and 2 cun to the side of the midline. Treats abdominal muscle spasm, bloated abdomen, and diarrhoea.

ST 25 TIANSHU
2 cun to the side of the centre of the navel. Treats pain in the abdomen, diarrhoea, constipation, vomiting, and irregular menstruation.

ST 29 GUILAI
4 cun below the centre of the navel and 2 cun to the side of the midline. Treats hernia, irregular menstruation, prolapse of the uterus, and male impotence.

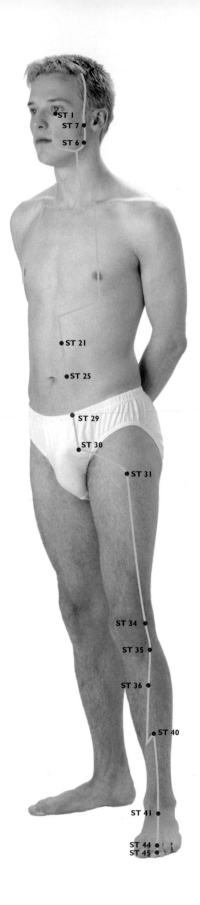

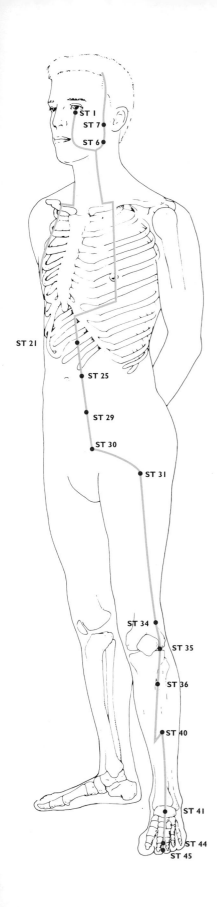

ST 31 BIGUAN
Below the front of the hip bone, level with the lower border of the pubic bone. Treats leg, hip, and abdominal pain.

ST 34 LIANGQIU
2 cun above the intersection of two lines – one across the top edge of the kneecap and the other along its outer edge. Treats knee pain, and stomach ache.

ST 35 DUBI
In the depression on the outer side of the knee, level with the lower edge of the kneecap. Treats knee pain and knee injuries.

ST 36 ZUSANLI
*3 cun below **ST 35** and 1 cun outside the crest of the tibia.* Treats stomach pain, gastric and duodenal ulcers, water retention, all types of prolapse of internal organs (in conjunction with **D 20**), diarrhoea and constipation, irregular menstruation, and knee pain. This point is one of the most powerfully effective of all. It strengthens the immune system, tonifies the Kidneys, and regulates the Spleen and Stomach, assisting in the digestion of food.

ST 40 FENGLONG
2 cun outside the crest of the tibia, 8 cun up the leg from the tip of the outer ankle bone. Treats phlegm, mucus congestion, and cough.

ST 41 JIEXI
In the middle of the crease formed in front of the ankle joint when the foot is bent upward. Treats ankle joint pain, both chronic and acute, and frontal headaches.

ST 44 NEITING
Between the 2nd and 3rd toes just above the web. Treats the same conditions as **ST 41** but more powerfully.

The Metal Element

The Lung is the yin Organ influenced by the energies of the Metal Element. The Large Intestine is its paired yang Organ.

CASE STUDY

Susan, aged 60, has caught another cold and cough. She has mild asthma and her chest feels very tight. Her nose always feels blocked and she uses an inhaler to help her breathing. As a baby she had eczema and now her skin is very dry. Susan gets on badly with her son-in-law and as a result hardly sees her grandchildren. This disappoints her and causes her great sadness.

Susan's problems with her nose, and her dry skin indicate an imbalance in the Metal energies of the Lungs and Large Intestine Organs. A blockage in Lung Qi affects normal respiration, causing coughs and a blocked nose. Her feelings of sadness indicate an imbalance in Lung Qi. Susan should have Tui Na on the neck, shoulders, and arms, concentrating on the Large Intestine and Lung Meridians and also on the *Shu* point for the Lung, **BL 13** (see page 24). All of these points give access to Lung Qi.

THE LUNG ORGAN

- takes in pure Qi from the air
- gives out impure Qi
- transforms Qi into a form usable by the body
- encourages the descent of Qi and Body Fluids to all parts of the body, particularly to the Kidneys
- influences the production of urine
- affects overall water balance
- opens into the nose
- is related to grief

THE LARGE INTESTINE ORGAN

- controls the downward progression of food residues from the Small Intestine
- absorbs water into the body

THE LUNG MERIDIAN

Treatment on Lung Meridian Qi-points is recommended for:
- lung problems, coughing, asthma, chest pain
- sore throat
- thumb pain

LARGE INTESTINE MERIDIAN

Treatment on Large Intestine Meridian Qi-points is recommended for:
- problems on the front of the head and face: toothache, headache, nasal congestion
- relieving a high temperature
- pain on the front of the shoulder joint
- tennis elbow
- repetitive strain injury of wrist, hand, or thumb

Lung Meridian

The Lung Meridian starts at **LU 1**, level with the space between the first and second ribs and 6 *cun* from the midline. It ends at **LU 11** on the outside of the thumb.

LU 2 YUNMEN
In a depression under the collar bone 6 cun from the chest midline. Treats coughs.

LU 5 CHIZE
On the elbow crease just outside the tendon of the biceps muscle. Treats lung problems, coughing, sore throat, fever, and elbow pain.

LU 6 KONGZUI
5 cun down the arm from ***LU 5,*** *on the inner edge of the radius.* Treats acute attacks of asthma and coughing.

LU 7 LIEQUE
1.5 cun above the middle wrist crease, in a small depression just above the small bony lump (styaloid process) on the thumb side. Treats fever, coughs, headache, and also neck pain (accessed through the paired Large Intestine Meridian).

LU 9 TAIYUAN
On the main wrist crease just inside the large tendon that runs down to the thumb. Treats asthmatic cough, wrist pain and numbness, and any soreness along the Lung Meridian.

LU 10 YUJI
Just under the midpoint of the first metacarpal bone (at the base of the thumb). Treats asthma attacks, sore throats, thumb pain.

LU 11 SHAOSHANG
At the outside margin of the thumb just behind the nail. Treats sore throat.

LU 1 ZHONGFU
2 cun below ***LU 2*** *level with the space between the first and second ribs.* Treats coughs and chesty colds.

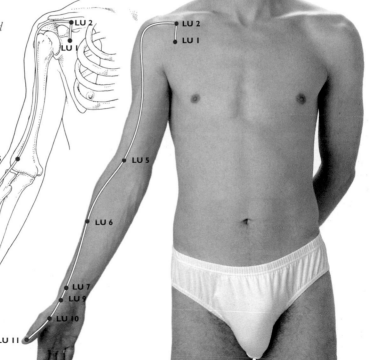

Large Intestine Meridian

This Meridian starts at **LI 1** on the thumb side of index finger just
behind the nail, and runs along the arm to the face, ending
at **LI 20** on the outside
of the nostril.

LI 20 YINGXIANG
In the depression on the side of the nostril. Treats
nasal discharge and rhinitis, sinusitis, and
facial paralysis.

LI 14 BINAO
*On a line from **LI 11** to **LI 15**
level with the lower end of the
deltoid muscle.* Treats upper
arm pain and stiffness in
the deltoid region.

LI 15 JIANYU
*In a depression on the front top edge of the shoulder
found when the arm is bent at the elbow and held
up horizontally.* Treats pain and stiffness of
the shoulder joint.

LI 11 QUCHI
*At the outer end of the elbow crease
when the arm is flexed.* Treats
fever associated with flu and
colds, skin conditions such as
eczema and urticaria (hives),
gastric spasms, abdominal pain
and diarrhoea, tennis elbow,
and high blood pressure.

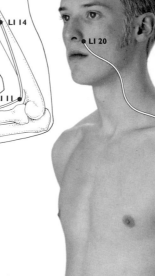

LI 10 SHOUSANLI
*2 cun down from **LI 11**.* Treats tennis elbow, stomach
and intestinal pain, indigestion, and diarrhoea.

LI 4 HEGU
*At the base of the V formed between the metacarpals of
thumb and index finger.* This point is one of the most
powerful for general wellbeing and stimulating the
immune system. Treats most head and face
problems particularly headaches, toothache, nasal
discharge, congestion and poor hearing, local pain
in the thumb, constipation, and numbness in the
hand.
Caution: do not use this point during pregnancy.

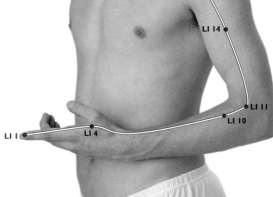

The Water Element

The Kidney is the yin Organ influenced by the energies of the Water Element. The Bladder is the paired yang Organ.

THE KIDNEY ORGAN

- stores Original Jing (see page 16) and refined essence from food
- dominates the development processes and all reproductive functions
- determines the strength of the constitution
- controls water balance
- sends pure fluids to the Lung via the Spleen
- excretes impure fluids as urine
- dominates energy transformation
- provides body heat
- receives Qi from the Lungs and holds it in the lower body
- controls the production of marrow, Blood, bones, and teeth
- controls brain function and the will
- opens into the ears
- affects hair health
- is related to fear

CASE STUDY

Madeline has severe lower back pain and a numbing ache in the back of her leg. She has two small children – a year-old son who is not yet walking, and a toddler whom she is potty training – and all the bending and carrying aggravates her back pain. She does not get enough sleep and constantly feels exhausted. Recently she has also been aware of a slight ringing sound in her ears. Madeline has always tended to backache, and her doctor has prescribed painkillers and rest.

Madeline's symptoms indicate an imbalance in the Water energies of the Kidney and Bladder. Her lower back pain, exhaustion, and ear problems suggest a Kidney Qi imbalance. The Bladder Meridian, which gives access to Kidney Qi, passes through the lower back and down the back of the legs. Madeline should have Tui Na on the lower back and legs, and on the *Shu* point for the Kidney, **BL 23** (see page 24).

THE BLADDER ORGAN

- receives and stores urine, under the control of the Kidney

THE KIDNEY MERIDIAN

Treatment on Kidney Meridian Qi-points is recommended for:
- lower back pain
- asthma
- oedema
- pain in the back of the knee
- cold hands and feet

THE BLADDER MERIDIAN

Treatment on Bladder Meridian Qi-points is recommended for:
- eye problems
- pain in the lower back, back of the legs, and outer ankle
- cramps
- urinary problems
- problems with any Organ, through the *Shu* points of the back (see page 24)

Kidney Meridian

The Kidney Meridian starts at **K 1** on the sole of the foot and ends on **K 27** which is in a depression on the lower edge of the collarbone 2 *cun* to the side of the midline.

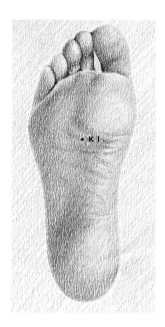

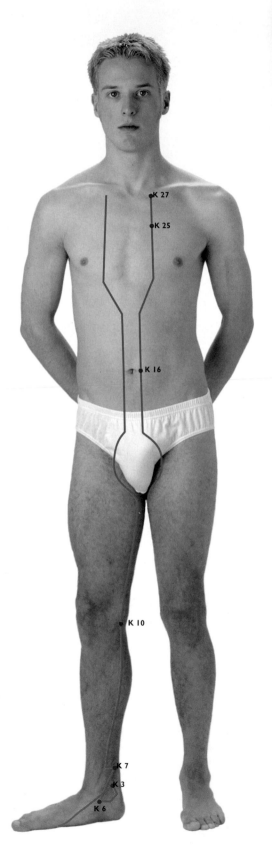

K 1 YONGQUAN
In a depression on the midline of the sole, two-thirds along from the back of the heel. Treats fainting (by restoring consciousness), shock, restless mind, epilepsy, infantile convulsion, and severe pain such as toothache. Health Care point (see p. 24) for sleep and appetite.

K 3 TAIXI
Midway between the tip of the inner ankle bone and the Achilles tendon. An important point for Qi deficiency of the Kidney. Treats lower back pain, excessive frequency of urination, tinnitus, poor vision, insomnia, and irritability.

K 6 ZHAOHAI
In a small depression directly below the centre of the inner ankle bone. Treats the same conditions as **K 3**.

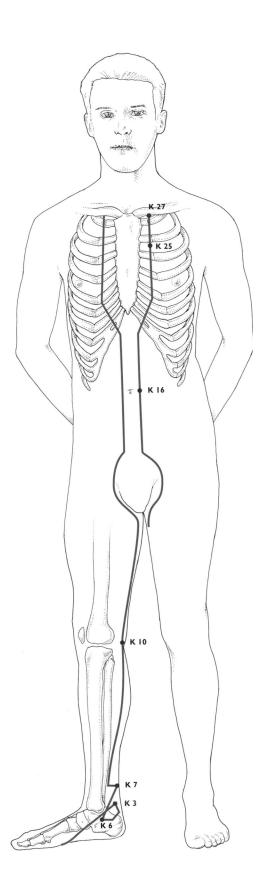

K 25 SHENCANG
In the space between the 2nd and 3rd ribs, level with LU 1, and 2 cun out from the midline. Treats coughs, asthma, heart stress, and calms the mind.

K 16 HUANGSHU
0.5 cun to the side of the navel. Treats abdominal pain and diarrhoea.

K 10 YINGU
On the back knee crease in the dimple toward the inner margin of the knee. Treats knee ligament problems.

K 7 FULIU
2 cun directly above K 3. Treats oedema and excessive night sweating.

Bladder Meridian

This is the longest Meridian, starting on the inner corner of the eye and ending at **BL 67** on the outer edge of the little toe, just behind the nail. The *Shu* points are on this Meridian (see page 24).

BL 10 TIANZHU
1.3 cun to the side of the midline just below the base of the skull. Sustained, deep pressure relaxes tense muscles below the base of the skull, easing pain and stiffness.

BL 11 DASHU Bone Point
1.5 cun from the midline, level with the lower border of the spinous process of thoracic vertebra 1. Helps clear Qi blockages in bones and joints of the neck, shoulder, and back.

BL 13 FEISHU Lung Point
1.5 cun from the midline, level with the lower border of the spinous process of thoracic vertebra 3. Regular deep pressure promotes healthy lungs; treats asthma and bronchial coughs.

BL 15 XINSHU Heart Point
1.5 cun from the midline, level with the lower border of the spinous process of thoracic vertebra 5. Treats all kinds of heart conditions, anaemia, epilepsy, chest tightness, and insomnia. Calms the mind.

BL 17 GESHU Blood Point
1.5 cun from the midline, level with the lower border of the spinous process of thoracic vertebra 7. Treats all kinds of blood problems including deficiencies and bleeding; also urticaria (hives).

BL 18 GANSHU Liver Point
1.5 cun from the midline, level with the lower border of the spinous process of thoracic vertebra 9. Treats liver problems including jaundice and hepatitis. Deep pressure relieves upper abdominal pain, blurred vision, and night blindness. The Gall Bladder Point **BL 19**, on the lower margin of thoracic vertebra 10, complements the effects of **BL 18**.

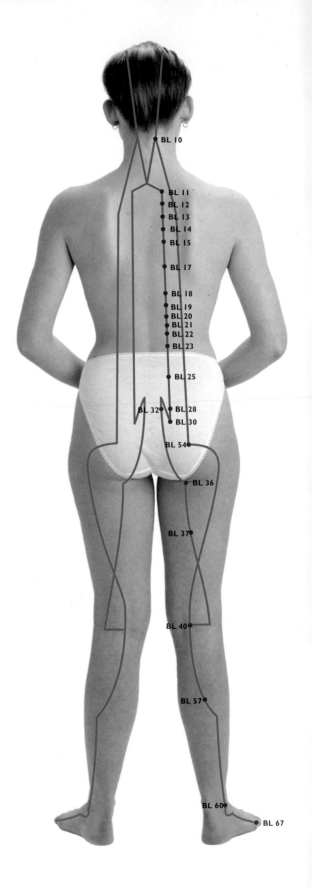

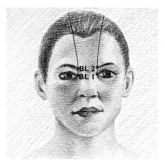

BL 2 ZANZHU
On the inner tip of the eyebrow. Treats sore eyes and frontal headache.

BL 20 PISHU Spleen Point
1.5 cun from the midline, level with the lower border of the spinous process of thoracic vertebra 11. Keeps Spleen function healthy; regular pressure relieves tiredness, lack of energy, indigestion; relieves vomiting, diarrhoea, hiccups, and jaundice. **BL 21,** the Stomach Point, is on the lower border of thoracic vertebra 12, and complements its effects.

BL 23 SHENSHU Kidney Point
1.5 cun from the midline, level with the lower margin of lumbar vertebra 2. Enhances Kidney function; essential for treating chronic lower backache. Eases ear problems such as tinnitus and poor hearing.

BL 25 DACHANGSHU Large Intestine Point
1.5 cun from the midline, level with the lower margin of lumbar vertebra 4. Affects Qi-flow in lumbar, sacral, and buttock regions, relieving pain, especially sciatica. Regulates the Large Intestine and treats diarrhoea and constipation.

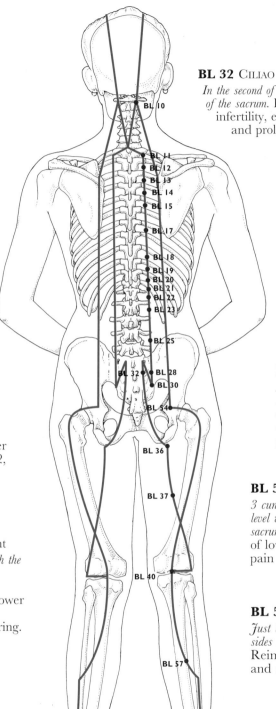

BL 32 CILIAO
In the second of the 4 depressions on either side of the sacrum. Eases lumbago; treats infertility, excessive vaginal discharge, and prolapse of the uterus in women.

BL 36 CHENGFU
In the middle of the crease below the buttock. Relieves sciatic pain and numbness in the legs.

BL 37 YINMEN
*On the midline of the back of the thigh, halfway between **BL 36** and the knee crease.* Treats lower back pain, sciatica, and paralysis of lower leg.

BL 40 WEIZHONG·
At the midpoint of the crease behind the knee joint. Treats acute spasm and pain in the calf muscles and controls the pain from lumbar strain.

BL 54 ZHIBIAN
3 cun to the side of the midline and level with the lower border of the sacrum. Essential for the treatment of lower backache, sciatica, and pain in the heel.

BL 57 CHENGSHAN
Just below the point where the two sides of the calf muscle meet. Reinforces the effects of **BL 40** and treats acute pain in the calf.

BL 60 KUNLUN
In the depression between the outer ankle bone and the Achilles tendon. Treats sprained ankle pain and heel problems; relieves headaches, lower back pain, and sciatica.

Ren Meridian

The Meridian starts at **R 1**, midway between the anus and the genitals, and runs up the front of the body to end at **R 24**, on the midline below the lower lip. **Caution:** do not use **R 3** and **R 4** during pregnancy.

*The **Ren** and **Du** Meridians are the two unpaired Meridians. Together they encircle the head and trunk along the midline.*

R 17 TANZHONG

On the sternum level with the space between the 4th and 5th ribs. Treats cardiac pain, chest pain, asthma, and coughing. Has a calming effect.

R 12 ZHONGWAN

4 cun above the navel. Treats gastric pain, vomiting, nausea, flatulence, and hiccups.

R 6 QIHAI

1.5 cun below the navel. Intensifies Qi function throughout the body. Treats prolapse of internal organs, Kidney weakness, and all Qi deficiency.

R 3 ZHONGJI

1 cun above the pubic bone. Treats urine retention and dribbling, impotence, seminal emission, irregular menstruation, and reproductive system problems.

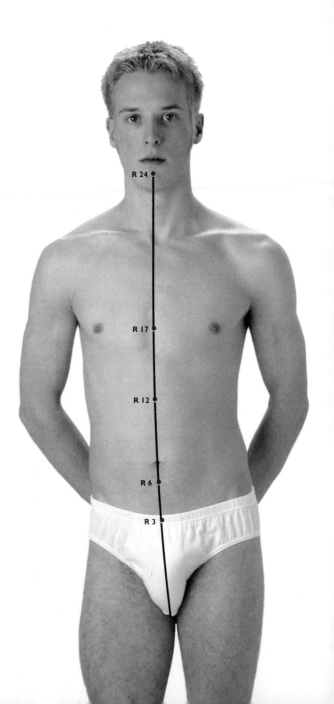

Du Meridian

D 1 is midway between the tip of the coccyx and the anus. The Meridian ends at **D 28,** inside the mouth at the junction of the gum and upper lip.

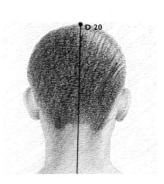

D 26 RENZHONG
Two-thirds of the way up the furrow between the nose and lip. Restores consciousness.

D 20 BAIHUI
At the top of the head, midway between the ears. Treats all kinds of headaches, dizziness, and prolapses (in conjunction with **ST 36**).

D 14 DAZHUI
In the midline between cervical vertebra 7 and thoracic vertebra 1. Six yang Meridians meet here. Treats asthma, epilepsy, and schizophrenia.

D 4 MINGMEN
In the midline between lumbar vertebrae 2 and 3. Treats lower back pain and lumbago.

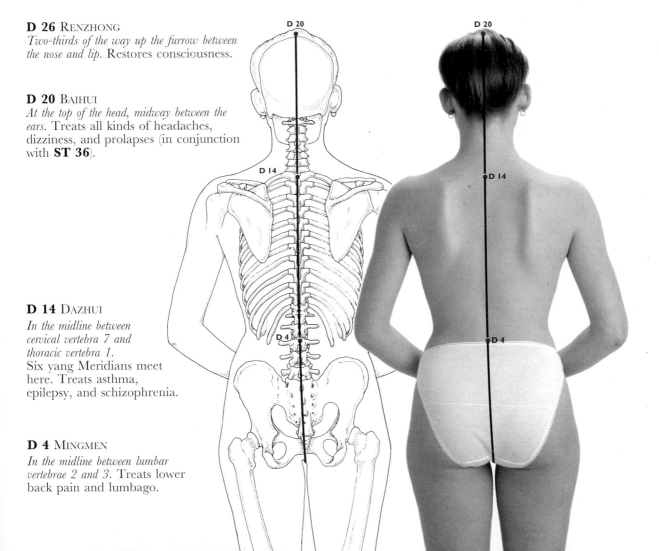

Chapter Four

Tui Na techniques

This chapter describes the techniques used in Tui Na, and the particular effects of each one. You will need to use these techniques in the whole-body routine described in Chapter Five. To familiarize yourself with them, study the photographs and read the instructions. You can then go on to practise the techniques either on yourself, or on a partner who should be seated comfortably in an upright chair, or lying on a firm surface. Take turns to practise on each other, so that you know how it feels to receive Tui Na, as well as to give it. Through practising these techniques with a partner you will be able to experience the benefits of the exchange of Qi energy between you, which is an important element of Tui Na.

The "soft tissue" techniques, which work on the muscles and underlying tissues, are presented first, on pages 54–67. Techniques for joint manipulation follow on pages 68–79. All these techniques stimulate the flow of Qi in different ways and also allow the exchange of Qi between giver and receiver.

Before you start to practise Tui Na, consider whether your partner has any conditions that are contraindicated. These were described in Chapter One. In particular:
• Do not use Tui Na on anyone with severe heart disease, osteoporosis, or cancer, especially of the skin and lymphatic system.
• Do not massage directly on the lower back or abdomen of a pregnant woman.
• Do not use Qi-points **SP 6** or **LI 4** during pregnancy.
• Do not massage directly on inflamed or broken skin, eczema, psoriasis, or shingles.

The techniques are presented in groups, such as squeezing, kneading, and pressing. Within each group there are variations; for example, for squeezing you can use the whole hand, the finger and thumb, or both hands interlocked. Many of the techniques have specific effects on underlying tissues such as muscle relaxation, stimulation of blood flow, or lymph drainage. The lymphatic system helps the body deal with infection and relies on such muscle movement to keep the lymph flowing. Some techniques act on Qi-points in the same way as acupuncture, releasing blockage, stimulating flow, and clearing stagnation. The most important benefits of the techniques are listed for each group.

Whatever kind of massage therapy you practise, when you first start rubbing a tense, knotted muscle, it hurts. Only with repeated hard and concentrated rubbing will the muscle release its tension and the pain subside. In Tui Na, the Qi-points being massaged are often tender – indeed, this is a good guide to their position – and initial kneading may be uncomfortable. Your partner needs to know this, and that Tui Na uses strong physical forces to affect Qi-flow and joint function.

Begin every technique with fairly gentle pressure and increase it gradually. Talk to your partner throughout and be guided by any reaction. If there is pain, is it a "good" pain, or should you stop? Always be ready to reduce the pressure you use, or change to a gentler technique.

Soft tissue techniques
pages 54-67

The soft tissue massage techniques all apply pressure to the underlying tissues – muscles, ligaments, tendons, and blood vessels. This pressure is applied in a variety of ways: at right angles to the body; in a circular motion; or with a shearing motion across the underlying muscles.

Apply the pressure by leaning in to your working arm with your body weight. The amount of pressure can be varied enormously, depending on the part of your body you use, and the amount of body weight you lean into the movement. To feel this, sit in an upright chair and press with your whole hand on your thigh. Then, without changing the amount of force you are using, move your hand so that you are pressing just with the thumb. Using your thumb you are pressing over a smaller area, so the pressure is greater. If you rock the thumb over and back, keeping the end of it pressed on one point, or if you rotate the heel of the palm over a point, you apply a different kind of pressure again.

Always start with gentle pressure and increase it gradually, releasing it equally gradually as you finish the technique. Where the techniques use one hand only, use your dominant hand. For some of the steps in the sequence the techniques are described for one side of the body only. To treat the other side, reverse right and left in the instructions.

In the techniques that follow, "you" refers to the giver, and "your partner" to the receiver.

Pressing

Pressing is basic to all Tui Na techniques. Using the palm, the heel of the hand, the elbow, the thumb, and even the foot, a skilled therapist will apply precisely the right amount of pressure to the area being treated. When you use pressing, progress steadily from light to heavier pressure, guided by your partner's response.

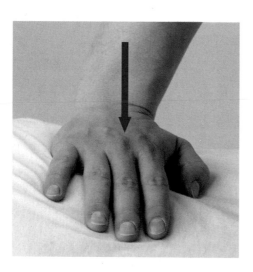

PALM PRESS
A simple press uses only one hand, with the palm on your partner's body and fingers together. Bring your body weight over the hand to generate pressure, gently at first, increasing gradually. Apply greater pressure by using the heel of the palm which covers a smaller area, thus focusing the force more intensely. This is ideal for thickly muscled areas such as buttocks and thighs.

DOUBLE PALM PRESS
Use both hands simultaneously to apply pressure either to adjacent or to distant areas. For some treatments the palms press in opposition to each other, such as on either side of the head.

CROSSED PALM PRESS
Press the fingers and palm of the free hand on the back of the working hand. This gives greater pressure with more precise control.

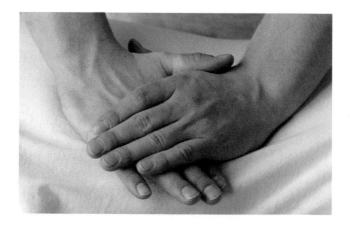

THUMB PRESS

This kind of press can apply the most concentrated pressure for a given force. If it hurts you to maintain strong pressure with the thumb, try using the tip of the elbow. When even deeper pressure is required, press the free thumb down on top of the working one.

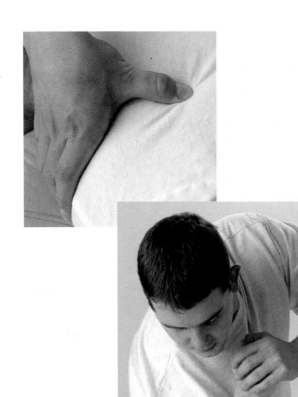

ELBOW PRESS

This press concentrates the force on to the area being treated so that greater pressure can be applied. For gentler pressure use your upper forearm instead.

BENEFITS OF PRESSING
- stimulates the sense organs in the skin
- aids Qi-flow through underlying tissues
- stimulates the flow of lymph
- pressing with the thumb or elbow has acupuncture-like effects on specific Qi-points
- stimulates Qi exchange between partners
- relieves pain

Squeezing

The "Na" in Tui Na is translated from the Chinese as squeezing, pinching, grasping, pulling, or grabbing. In a squeeze the tissues are held in a way that subjects them to pressures from opposite directions. Every squeeze pulls or lifts up to some extent the area being massaged. As for all techniques involving deep pressure, you should begin the squeeze gently and increase it gradually.

WHOLE HAND SQUEEZE
The fingers press toward the heel of the palm, creating opposing pressures. This squeeze covers a larger area than finger-and-thumb squeezes, generating deep but more diffuse pressure. Use both hands simultaneously to give greater coverage.

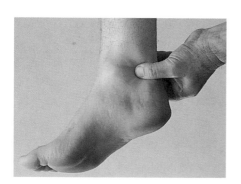

FINGER AND THUMB SQUEEZE
A simple squeeze uses thumb and index and/or middle finger, but using all the fingers gives added strength to oppose the thumb pressure. This squeeze can produce very deep and concentrated pressure on specific Qi-points.

INTERLOCKED HAND SQUEEZE
With one hand on either side of the limb being
treated, interlock your fingers over the top.
Squeeze to apply strong opposing pressure from
the heels of the hands.

BENEFITS OF SQUEEZING
● stimulates blood flow
● stimulates lymph flow
● strongly affects Qi-flow
● helps loosen adjacent muscles
● affects the connective tissue sheath
around the muscles

Kneading

Kneading involves pressing with movement. Unlike rubbing, your hand (or elbow) must not slide on your partner's skin. The kneading movement may be to and fro or circular, and is limited only by the looseness of your partner's skin. A skilled therapist can create a range of different pressures delivered with subtle nuances of direction and force. The Chinese use the fleshy heel of the thumb (the "fish belly") when kneading on the face. Kneading can produce very gentle, relaxing pressure, or very deep stimulation. The massage effect results from the skin moving with pressure over the underlying tissues.

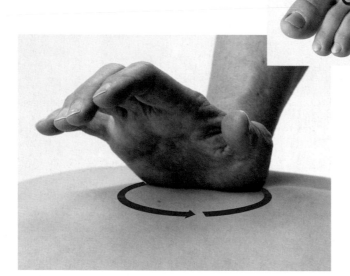

THUMB KNEADING
Here the thumb moves in a circle to apply a penetrating pressure; the rest of the hand supports the thumb. Thumb kneading applies a very concentrated stimulus to a Qi-point or a knotted area of soft tissue.

HEEL OF THE THUMB
This uses the fleshy area at the base of the thumb. It is gentler than heel of the hand kneading, and much less intense than thumb kneading.

HEEL OF THE HAND
Rock the heel of the hand to and fro, or move it in a circle. This technique covers a larger area than thumb kneading, but with less pressure.

BENEFITS OF KNEADING
- relieves tension in groups of muscles
- assists the flow of Blood
- stimulates the drainage of lymph to help flush away toxins
- assists relaxation
- creates favourable conditions in the tissues for the diffusion and balance of Qi

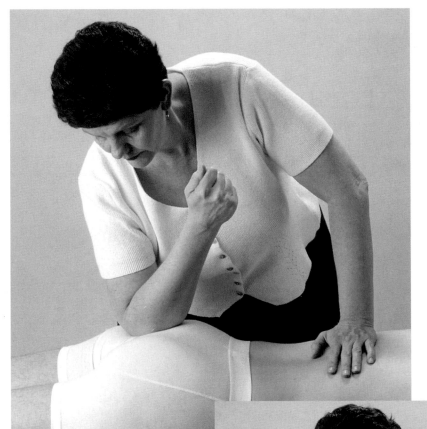

ELBOW KNEADING

This is the same as the elbow press (p. 55) but with to and fro or circular motion. Increase the pressure gently, since very deep pressure can be generated if too much body weight is used. Full pressure with the tip of the elbow is usually only used on Qi-point **GB 30** on the buttocks, but can be used on **GB 21** if your partner is stronger than you.

FOREARM KNEADING

For less penetrating pressure, use the upper third of the fore-arm instead of the tip of the elbow. You can sit, resting the hand and wrist. Both elbow and forearm kneading are good for buttock and thigh massage.

Rubbing

The Chinese describe rubbing techniques as pushing, scrubbing, chafing, pressing, and dragging. Rubbing involves movement over the skin surface, creating friction which generates heat. It can vary from a very gentle to and fro movement to a vigorous scrubbing. Rubbing can be in a line or a circle, and involves larger sized movements than those used in kneading.

PALMAR RUB

The palm makes circular or to and fro rubbing movements over the body, as many as 100 times a minute. Although the pressure is light, this rub is very relaxing and stimulates blood circulation to the skin. Using the heel of the hand or the thumb makes rubbing more vigorous and penetrating, though it is never deep enough to cause pain.

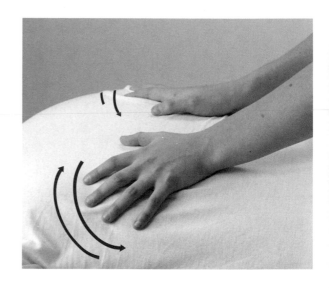

CHAFING

This is rubbing with the outer edge of the hand. It is done on bare skin, using a little massage oil to prevent soreness. Make long, precise strokes with a fast sawing motion along the lines of the Meridians. Alternatively you can use shorter and more rapid strokes in the lumbar region, where its powerful warming effect stimulates the flow of Qi.

TWO-HAND CHAFING

Here both hands act like saws, moving in opposite directions. Chafing across the sacral area of the lower back, for instance, generates heat which your partner may feel along the lines of the Bladder Meridian of the legs even as far as the feet.

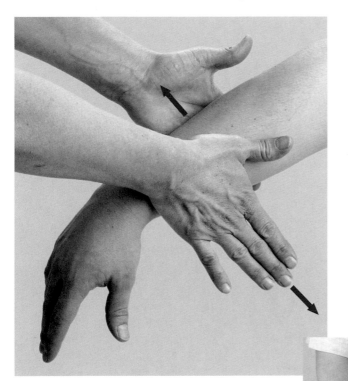

PALMS IN OPPOSITION

This technique gives a vigorous rubbing with the palms on both sides of arms, legs, fingers, thumbs, and shoulders. Begin at the top of a limb and move downward gradually.

UPPER FOREARM RUB

Here both forearms rub simultaneously in opposite directions. Use this technique on the back, covering the whole spine, and working from the centre outward and back again. Give a push on the outward movement to effect a slight stretch.

BENEFITS OF RUBBING
● generates warmth, stimulating circulation
● promotes flow of Qi in surface tissues

Stroking

Stroking is similar to rubbing, but with the movement in one direction only. Some stroking techniques are deep and vigorous.

PALMAR STROKING

This is a long rub in one direction, more like a surface push than conventional stroking. It is the "Tui" part of Tui Na. The hands follow the course of the Meridians with a strong feeling for the energy being moved. The stroking action is usually away from the centre of the body.

THUMB STROKE

Both thumbs stroke outward from the midline.

BENEFITS OF STROKING
● moves Qi through surface tissues
● stimulates the flow of lymph
● induces a feeling of relaxation

Vibration

For this technique the hand quivers, sending vibrations into the tissues and facilitating the exchange of Qi between you and your partner.

Holding your palm flat on your partner's body, tense the muscles in your forearm while keeping your fingers loose, so that your hand quivers. This technique is mainly used on the abdomen.

BENEFITS OF VIBRATION
● stimulates Qi transfer to your partner

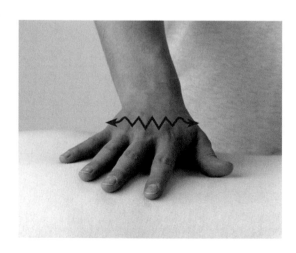

Thumb rocking

This technique applies penetrating thumb pressure on Qi-points.

First make sure your thumb nail is short. Put your thumb pad on the area to be treated and with a small to and fro movement of the forearm, rock your hand over the thumb so that it bends at the first joint. The overall effect is of bending and straightening the thumb rapidly whilst holding it on the same spot.

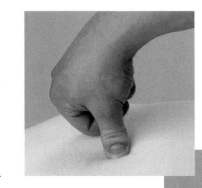

BENEFITS OF THUMB ROCKING
● produces acupuncture-like effects on Qi balance

Plucking

This technique is a shearing action, using very deep, controlled sideways movement across muscles or muscle groups.

Place the thumb pad flat on the skin, parallel to the muscle being treated. Now use the heel of the other hand to push the thumb backward and forward, kneading the muscle. Plucking works very well on muscles which are tightly knotted, and can feel quite painful at first.

BENEFITS OF PLUCKING
● relaxes the muscle
● promotes Qi-flow
● eases chronic pain

Rolling

Rolling is a fairly modern technique, only introduced this century, but it is very effective and important in Tui Na. Since it is difficult to learn from a book, an alternative version to Chinese rolling is also described here, which you may find easier. This is the BODYHARMONICS® roll, named after the therapy centre founded by the author.

Caution: do not use rolling on the face.

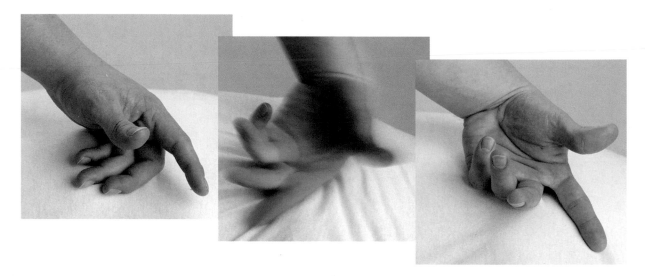

CHINESE ROLLING

In Chinese rolling the back of the hand rolls over the body. Press the outside edge of the back of the hand firmly against your partner's body, fingers held slightly apart and relaxed, as shown above, left. Keeping your wrist relaxed, rotate your forearm so that your hand flips smoothly backward. As your hand rolls across your partner's body it opens, so that the metacarpal region behind the knuckles and each knuckle in turn makes contact with the body

(see above, centre). The roll must be very smooth, with the hand always in contact with your partner's body. Do not allow the hand to flick up at the end of the roll. The return movement is also smooth, with the fingers loose, as if cradling an egg (see above, right).

Aim to make one complete movement per second, as anything slower than this will have little effect. An expert moves the hand like a rolling pin, making about 130 rolls per minute.

SINGLE BODYHARMONICS®
ROLLING

The BODYHARMONICS® roll is easier than the Chinese roll. Curl the fingers loosely with the thumb relaxed and put your hand on your partner's body, holding the top joints of the fingers and the nails against the area to be treated (see right). Roll the hand forward, as far as the knuckles (below, right). Then retract the forearm so the hand rolls back into the original position.

This roll is a simple to and fro motion created by a piston-like action of the forearm. Maintain an even pressure on the forward stroke as the backs of the fingers open out against the body. The hand should not rub, or lose contact with the skin.

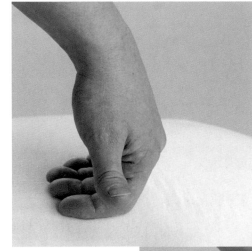

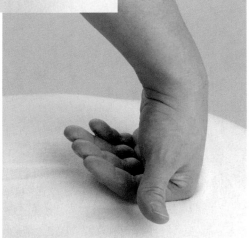

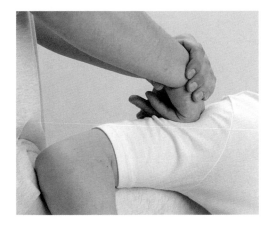

DOUBLE BODYHARMONICS® ROLLING

Place your free hand on top of the working one to increase the degree of penetration and help the rolling action.

BENEFITS OF ROLLING
- increases flow of Qi
- stretches muscles and tendons
- aids relaxation
- helps to balance Qi

Percussion

These percussive techniques apply pressure for a very short time; the amount of pressure depends on the force used and the area over which it is applied. Percussion is mostly used to apply penetrating pressure to areas of the body with thick layers of muscle, such as the buttocks, the lumbar region, and the trapezius muscles across the shoulders.

PUMMELLING
Hold your hands in loose fists. Use the outer edges to pummel your partner's body with a rapid staccato action. Alternate your hands as you pummel.

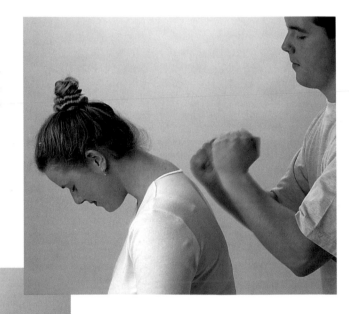

HACKING
Hold the hands with palms together and fingers spread. Strike the body with the sides of the hands, with the emphasis on the little fingers.

CUPPING

Hold the hand firmly in a cupped position. Allow the forearm to drop loosely with each stroke, the movement coming from the elbow. You can strike with some force because there is a cushion of air trapped between it and your partner's body.

When cupping on the back hold your hand *across* the sacral area but *lengthways* along the spine itself. This is a very good technique to use as a finale on flat, well muscled areas such as buttocks and thighs.

DOUBLE CUPPING

Cup both hands and hold them together so there is a cushion of air trapped between them. Striking lightly with the knuckles makes a soft noise which also has a therapeutic effect. This technique is used on the head.

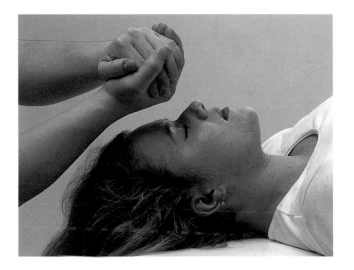

BENEFITS OF PERCUSSION
- aids muscle relaxation
- loosens ligaments and cartilage
- stimulates Blood and lymph circulation
- enhances the flow of Qi

Joint manipulation techniques *pages 68–79*

These techniques are safe to use to treat tired and aching joints. For serious joint pain you should always consult a trained practitioner or doctor.

Before using any joint manipulation technique, use soft tissue massage techniques on the area near the joint. This stimulates Qi and Blood flow, and relaxes muscles, tendons, and ligaments, enabling you to work on the joint safely and easily. When treating knees, for example, first use the soft tissue techniques suggested for the hips, leg, and foot in the whole-body routine in Chapter Five.

Always consider the physical limitations of the joint you are treating. The elbows and knees are hinge joints, allowing movement in one plane, though there is a little sideways movement in them. Only five joints in the body can rotate: the shoulders, the hips, and the neck. Of these, only the shoulder joint can rotate in a full circle. The wrist and ankle are sliding joints.

To assess a joint problem, first ask your partner to move the joint as far as possible and tell you where there is stiffness or pain. Manipulate slowly and smoothly, and stop if you feel resistance to what should be a normal movement.

The specific benefits are listed for each manipulation technique. Generally they relieve pain and stiffness in the joint capsule and the surrounding muscles. Contracted, tight muscles hold tension, which can be released by manipulation, allowing the muscles to lengthen and improving elasticity.

Shaking

The shake is used to treat the arms and legs. First loosen the muscles with a full soft tissue massage of the limbs. Shake only one arm at a time; the legs can be shaken together.

BENEFITS OF SHAKING
- extends the muscles surrounding the joint
- stimulates the flow of blood in the joint region
- improves the distribution of Qi in the tissues
- removes Qi blockages
- tones major muscles

ARM
- stimulates the tissues of the elbow joint capsule

DOUBLE LEG SHAKE
- helps prolapsed lumbar discs and sciatica
- helps release pressure between the vertebrae

SINGLE LEG SHAKE
- manipulates the hip joint

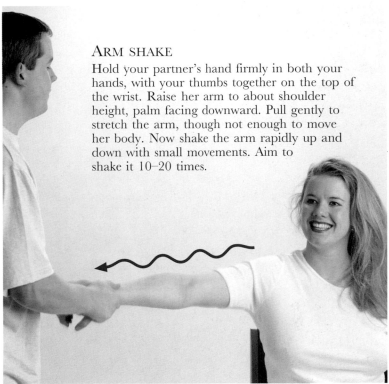

ARM SHAKE

Hold your partner's hand firmly in both your hands, with your thumbs together on the top of the wrist. Raise her arm to about shoulder height, palm facing downward. Pull gently to stretch the arm, though not enough to move her body. Now shake the arm rapidly up and down with small movements. Aim to shake it 10–20 times.

SINGLE LEG AND HIP SHAKE

With your partner lying on his back, place the fingers of both hands beneath the Achilles tendon and grasp the front of the ankle with the thumbs. Lift the leg up about one foot (30 cm). Pull on the leg gently and then shake it up and down rapidly with small movements. The shake should go right into the hip and the rest of the body. Aim to shake each leg 10–20 times.

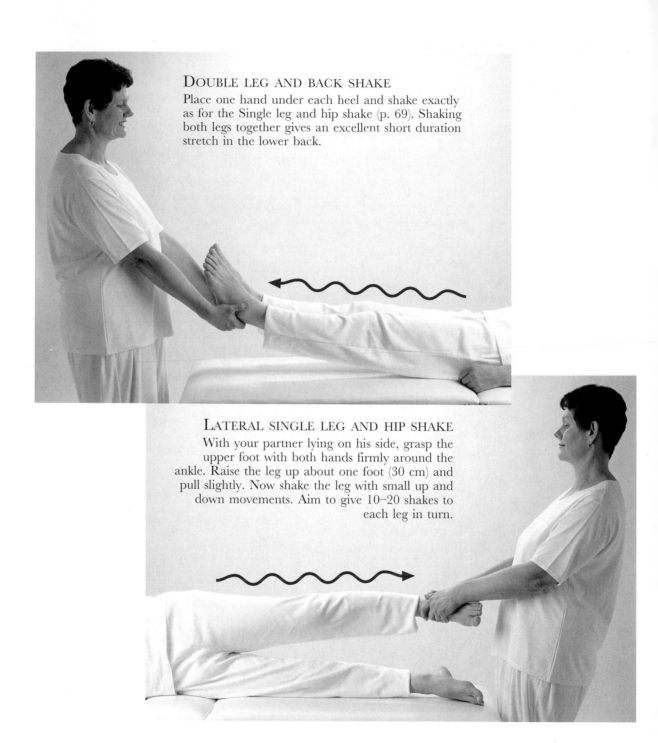

DOUBLE LEG AND BACK SHAKE
Place one hand under each heel and shake exactly as for the Single leg and hip shake (p. 69). Shaking both legs together gives an excellent short duration stretch in the lower back.

LATERAL SINGLE LEG AND HIP SHAKE
With your partner lying on his side, grasp the upper foot with both hands firmly around the ankle. Raise the leg up about one foot (30 cm) and pull slightly. Now shake the leg with small up and down movements. Aim to give 10–20 shakes to each leg in turn.

Extension and flexion

These techniques are used on hinge
joints – the elbow and the knee.

ELBOW EXTENSION AND FLEXION

Raise your partner's arm so that the elbow is level
with the lower ribs. Resting her elbow on the
fingers of your hand, press your thumb into **LI 11**
(see p. 44) just below the tendon of the biceps.

Holding her wrist with your other hand, firmly
flex and extend the arm, keeping your thumb on
LI 11. To increase the stimulation of the joint,
rotate the forearm slightly.

BENEFITS OF EXTENSION AND FLEXION
- aids joint mobility
- tendon stretches induce muscle relaxation
- improves joint function
- increases blood circulation in the joint tissues
- relieves "tennis elbow", knee, hip, and lower back pain

KNEE EXTENSION AND FLEXION

With your partner lying on his back, stand facing his leg. Cupping one hand under the heel and resting the other over the knee cap, lift the leg into the position shown above. With the hand under the heel, push the leg toward the body until you feel an acceptable degree of resistance. Now sharply push the knee and pull the heel, in the direction shown by the arrow above, to extend the leg. This manipulation improves flexibility in the knee and heel.

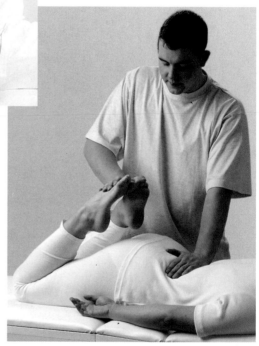

KNEE SUPER-FLEXION

With your partner lying on her front, stand level with her knees, holding your hands over the toes and their lower bones. Raise both her feet, flexing the knees. The aim is for the heels to touch the buttocks. Where there is extreme stiffness of the knee joint, flex one leg at a time. Adding a lumbar press, as shown above, manipulates the back as well as the knees and hips. For a stronger effect, repeat with the lower legs crossed, each way in turn.

Rotation

This techniques is for the shoulders, hip joints, ankles, and wrists. Do not attempt to rotate the neck, as it is easy to cause damage. The shoulder joint can rotate almost in a full circle, but its mobility varies enormously from one person to another. Even strong, healthy sportspeople may have severely restricted movement in shoulders and hips.

Always massage the soft tissues in the area before attempting a rotation, to aid the flow of blood and Qi and release muscle tension.

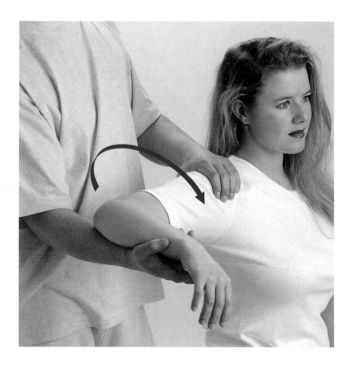

SHOULDER ROTATION WITH ELBOW FLEXED

Stand to the side and behind your partner, supporting her right forearm on yours with a light grip near the wrist. With your other hand grip the shoulder joint, pressing your middle finger into **LI 15** (p. 44) and your thumb into **SJ 14** (p. 36). With your right hand rotate the arm forward and backward. These circular movements should be as large as the mobility of the joint will allow.

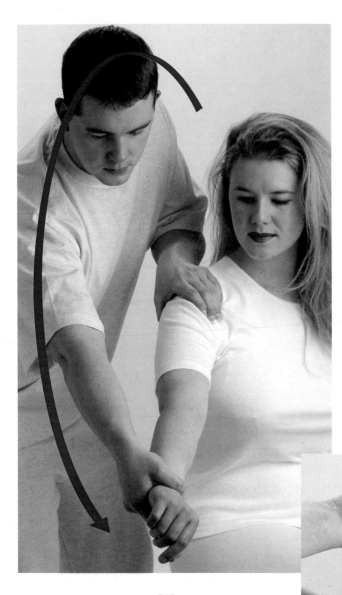

SHOULDER ROTATION WITH ELBOW EXTENDED

Extend the arm, holding it loosely by the wrist. With your left hand grip the shoulder joint, pressing your middle finger into **LI 15** (p. 44) and your thumb into **SJ 14** (p. 36). Then rotate the arm slowly, forward and backward, with large circular movements. Limit the size of the rotation if you feel any resistance.

WRIST ROTATION

With your partner's arm extended, support her wrist in one hand. With your other hand on her fingers, hold her hand in a vertical position. Rotate the wrist joint gently, clockwise and anticlockwise, as far as possible. A full wrist rotation may be painful if the wrist bones have ever been broken.

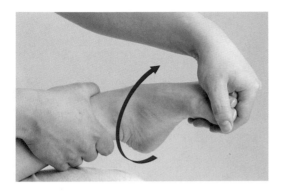

ANKLE ROTATION

With your partner lying on her back, raise the foot a little, supporting it with one hand under the ankle. With your other hand, grip the toes and rotate the foot, clockwise and anticlockwise.

HIP ROTATION

Flex your partner's right knee so that the lower leg is horizontal and supported across your right forearm. Grip the inside of the knee. Support the outside of the knee with the left hand, locking your fingers together over the top of the knee. Use your hands to rotate the hip carefully, making small circles clockwise and anticlockwise.

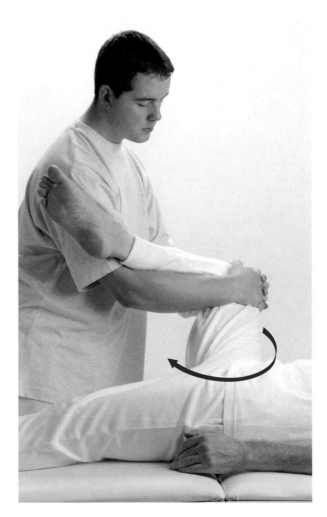

BENEFITS OF ROTATION
● aids mobility of the joints
● relieves pain in the joints
● frequent, gentle rotations benefit even severe arthritis

Pushing and pulling

These manipulations create two equal forces working in opposite directions: one "pulling" at a point distant from one "pushing". The techniques flex and twist the joints to a greater degree than normal, improving their mobility. Carefully control the amount of force you use, feeling for any resistance.

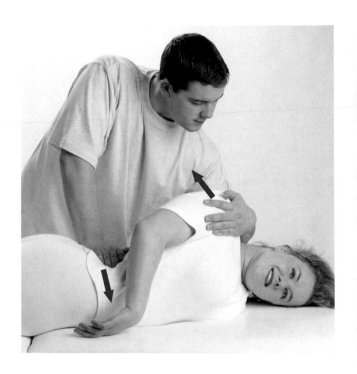

SHOULDER PULL WITH LUMBAR PUSH
With your partner lying face down, lean over from her left side and grasp her right shoulder with your left hand. At the same time press your right hand firmly down on the lumbar region, to the right of the spine. Now lift the shoulder while applying an equal but opposite force to the back. The result is a well controlled but potentially vigorous stretch of the front shoulder and upper chest, giving a twist to the lumbar and lower thoracic vertebrae.

BENEFITS OF PUSHING AND PULLING
● releases tension in muscled areas
● increases mobility of joints
● enhances body flexibility

SHOULDER PULL WITH SCAPULAR PRESS

This is similar to the Shoulder pull with lumbar push, but this time your partner's arm is flexed with her hand resting across her back. Raise her shoulder with your right hand, keeping your left hand tucked in against the edge of the right scapula, next to the spine. Pull and push with equal force to give a powerful shoulder stretch.

LEG LIFT WITH LUMBAR PRESS

With your partner lying face down, stand on his left, pressing your left hand onto **BL 25** on the side of the spine nearest you. Slide your right hand under the left leg, holding it just above the knee, and lift the leg as far as is comfortable. At the same time push with equal force on the lumbar area. Hold the lift for a few seconds, rotating the leg slightly before lowering it. From the same position, reach over and grasp the other leg to repeat on the opposite side.

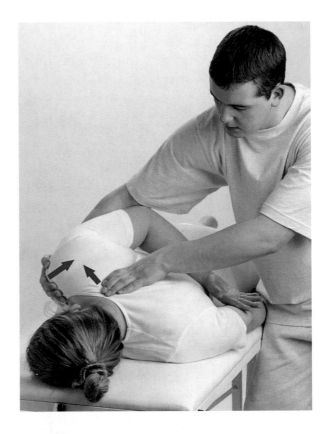

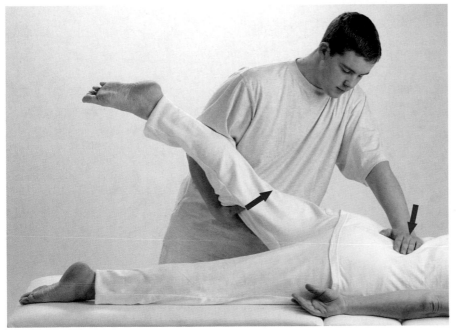

Stretching

These are spinal stretches which ease back
strain and relieve the pressure on damaged
intervertebral discs. Even those who have no
back problems find these stretches very
soothing and relaxing.

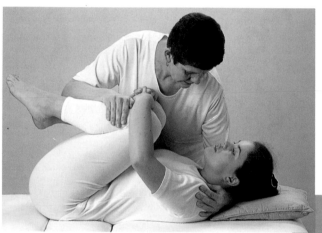

FOLDED BODY SPINAL STRETCH AND ROLL

Your partner lies on her back, hugging her
knees as near to her chest as possible. Stand on
her right side with your right hand and forearm
across her shins and your left arm under her
neck, grasping her left shoulder. Rock her forward on her back onto the buttocks, and back
again. Repeat the rocking action several times.

BENEFITS OF STRETCHING
FOLDED BODY SPINAL STRETCH AND ROLL
● relieves strain and spasm of the lower
back muscles
● relieves associated chronic pain

STANDING SPINAL STRETCH
● relieves lumbar conditions resulting in
limited backward flexion of the spine
● relieves chronic pain in the lumbar and
ilio-sacral regions

STANDING SPINAL STRETCH

Stand back to back with your partner, feet
slightly apart, and link arms. With her buttocks
above yours (flex your legs if necessary), bend
forward at the waist, and lift her off the floor so
her legs hang loosely. Shake her gently from side
to side, and lower her slowly to the floor.

Caution: do not attempt this if you have back
trouble, or with a partner much heavier or taller
than yourself.

Chapter Five

Whole-body routine

The unique whole-body Tui Na routine described in this chapter is a holistic treatment designed to increase energy and vitality, and promote health and wellbeing. This sequence of soft tissue techniques and joint manipulations balances Qi-flow, clearing blockages and stagnation. Unlike most other forms of holistic massage, Tui Na has a sound basis in Chinese medical theory. Clinically it is used to treat specific ailments and conditions. The routine presented here is a preventative treatment, which corrects any imbalances in the body's energy before symptoms and disease can develop. Since in Traditional Chinese Medicine the body, mind, and spirit are indivisible, the routine works to restore emotional and intellectual harmony, as well as physical health.

When you first start to practise Tui Na, concentrate on the steps of the routine that use the simpler techniques: rubbing, pressing, and squeezing. Refer back to the descriptions of the techniques in Chapter Four. For each step of the routine an illustration shows you the Meridians and Qi-points used. This will also help you to visualize the Meridians in the area you are massaging. For a fuller description of the positions and effects of the Qi-points, refer to the relevant Meridian illustration in Chapter Three.

The whole-body routine is divided into eight parts, each concentrating on a different area of the body and with your partner in a different position.

Partner seated
PART ONE: Neck and shoulder
PART TWO: Shoulder, arm, and hand

Partner lying face down
PART THREE: Back and hip
PART FOUR: Back of leg and foot

Partner lying on his or her side
PART FIVE: Lower back, hip, and leg

Partner lying on his or her back
PART SIX: Front of leg and foot
PART SEVEN: Abdomen and chest
PART EIGHT: Face, head, and neck

Work on each body area in the order shown, at least to begin with. When you are more experienced in giving Tui Na you can concentrate on parts of the body that need specific treatments, as suggested in Chapter Six. For example, you might give on-the-spot help to a partner suffering cramped muscles on the squash court, or a tension headache in the office, or even in a traffic jam. The routine described in this chapter, however, is meant to be carried out slowly and quietly in a relaxed atmosphere at home.

Preparation

To receive the full benefit from a Tui Na treatment your partner should be relaxed and calm. Before you start the whole-body routine, take time to prepare the room where you are going to work. Make sure it is warm, and comfortable; have a few small cushions or pillows ready to support your partner during treatment. Choose a quiet time and try to prevent interruptions from family, visitors, or the telephone. Adjust the lighting so that it is not too bright, which prevents relaxation of the eyes. You may also like to perfume the room using an essential oil burner, incense, or fresh flowers.

For the first part of the routine, seat your partner in a comfortable upright chair – such as a dining room chair – with good back support. Later in the routine your partner will need to lie down on a comfortable flat surface, such as a massage table. A sprung mattress or bed is not suitable because it will absorb the pressure you apply. If you do not have a massage table, you can use any table provided it is at hip height and large enough to lie on: about 6 feet by 2½ feet (180 cm by 80 cm). The table should be padded with

blankets and be positioned so that you can walk and move all around it. You need to be able to move freely when giving Tui Na, so wear loose, comfortable clothes and flat shoes or go barefoot. Remove all jewellery and ensure that your finger nails are short. Your partner should wear loose, thin clothes, preferably made from natural fibres. A cotton T-shirt and tracksuit trousers are ideal.

Before you start the routine, prepare your partner by explaining what you are going to do and how it might feel. Tui Na is vigorous and deep massage, and Qi-points can be tender, so encourage your partner to tell you how it feels as you go along. Ask where there is pain, and treat these areas thoroughly but with care. Never exert full pressure suddenly – always start with gentle pressure, increasing it gradually. Be guided by your partner on what is comfortable. Observe all the cautions given in Chapter One, and be careful to avoid any areas of bruising or broken skin. If your partner has a skin condition that prevents you massaging directly on some of the Qi-points, you can use distant points to complete the treatment (see page 22).

Allow at least one hour for the routine, especially while it is new to you. After a Tui Na treatment, both you and your partner should feel relaxed but at the same time energized. Allow your partner time to unwind after the treatment, especially if there has been a release of emotional tension.

Throughout the routine the instructions are given for a right-handed person. If you are left-handed you should reverse the positions given.

The Chinese character Qi highlights notes on the specific benefits of parts of the Tui Na routine.

PART ONE
Neck and shoulder

Part One deals largely with massage of the
muscles of the neck and shoulders, especially
the trapezius. Tui Na in this area releases
tension very effectively. Your partner should
be seated in a comfortable upright chair with
good middle back support.

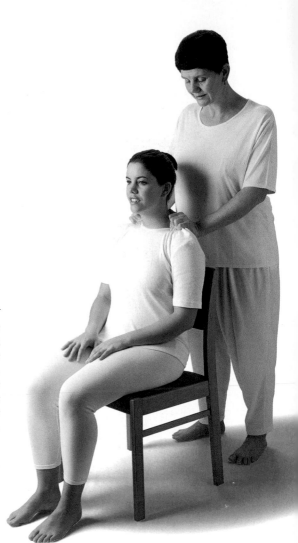

STEP 1   SQUEEZING AND KNEADING ▷

Standing behind your partner, stroke lightly along the
tops of the shoulders. Then squeeze gently along each
shoulder with the whole hand, gradually increasing the
pressure and starting to knead with the heel of the hand.
As you feel your partner begin to relax, knead with the
thumb, feeling for any tender or knotted tissue. Grasp the
top of the shoulder and squeeze the trapezius muscle
deeply, giving it a slight shake.

*These techniques unblock the energy
channels from the head to the shoulders,
raising energy levels significantly.*

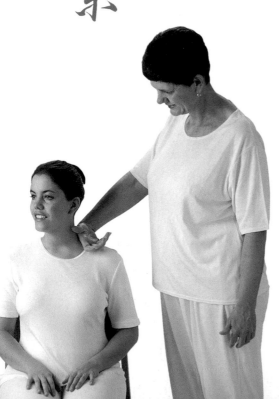

◁ STEP 2   CHINESE ROLLING

Standing behind your partner's left shoulder, start by
rolling with your right hand along the trapezius muscle
toward the base of the neck. Roll across this area for up
to 5 minutes, concentrating on the Gall Bladder and
Small Intestine Meridians. Repeat on the right shoulder
using your left hand and facing the back right of her
head. Repeat this rolling often during the routine.

*Rolling encourages the smooth flow of
Qi in the Meridians, harmonizing the
body's internal energy, and creating a
radiant feeling of wellbeing.*

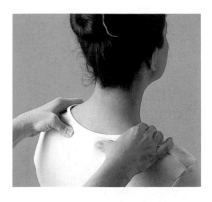

◁ STEP 3 PRESSING AND KNEADING QI-POINTS

Repeat the squeezing and kneading of Step 1 but now press and knead with the thumb on **GB 21**, **SI 9–14**, and **BL 11**, **13**, and **15**. Knead each point for at least 30 seconds, gradually increasing the pressure.

Pressure applied to specific Qi-points on the Meridians usually causes some discomfort, but is necessary to release tension.

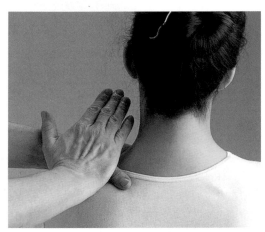

◁ STEP 4 PLUCKING ON THE SHOULDER

Place your left thumb on your partner's left shoulder with your fingers lying over the top. Using the heel of your right hand over the thumb pluck across **GB 21,** pushing toward the neck. Repeat on the right shoulder, fingers downward across the right shoulder blade.

*Plucking **GB 21** balances the energy and benefits the muscles and bones of the neck region. This simple method of relaxing knotted tissue gives a blissfully light feeling.*

MAIN QI-POINTS FOR NECK AND SHOULDER MASSAGE
These are found on the Bladder Meridian (shown in blue), Small Intestine Meridian (red), and Gall Bladder Meridian (green).

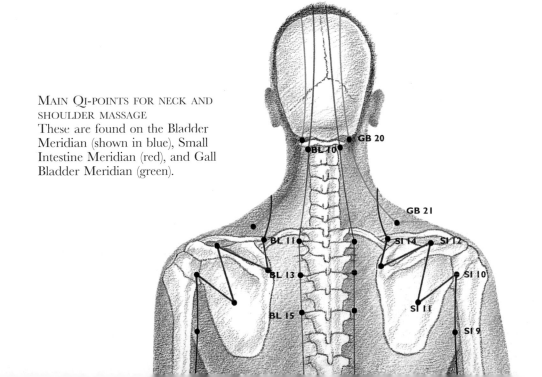

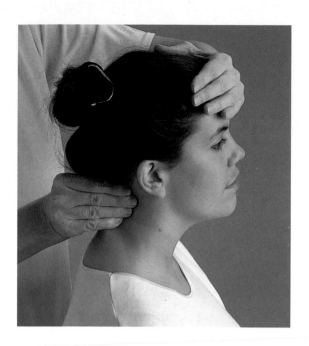

◁ STEP 5   SQUEEZING AND KNEADING

Using your thumb and first two fingers, squeeze the muscles on either side of the neck vertebrae while the other hand lightly supports the forehead. Progress from light to strong pressure with a definite kneading action. Work from the base of the neck up to the region just beneath the skull, lifting the hand between each position. Change hands frequently.

 This technique stimulates the Bladder and Gall Bladder Meridians, sweeping away the tension which leads to headaches and relieving stiff and aching neck muscles.

STEP 6   KNEADING QI-POINTS WITH PRESSURE

With the thumb and middle finger on **GB 20** and **BL 10,** press diagonally upward toward the eyes. Squeeze and knead each point for 20–30 seconds at a time, then change hands and repeat.

 GB 20 *is one of the best Qi-points for treating headaches on the front of the head. It also affects the eyes, ears, nose, and mouth.* ***BL 10*** *relaxes stiff necks and can help tired and sore eyes.*

STEP 7   PERCUSSION ON THE SHOULDERS ▷

Use the pummelling technique on the top of the shoulders and either side of the spine near the shoulder blades. Hacking has a similar effect.

 Pummelling is intensely exhilarating and unblocks Qi energy as well as moving blood and lymph.

PART TWO

Shoulder, arm, and hand

The first steps work on the right side of the body; steps for the left follow on page 94.

steps for the left follow on page 94.

STEP 1   ROLLING THE FRONT SHOULDER ▷

Standing on your partner's right, put your right foot on the chair so your thigh is about level with her armpit. With your left hand, grasp her right wrist and raise the arm so that it lies out across your knee. Turn the wrist away from you to expose the deltoid muscle on the front shoulder. Then roll with your right hand up this muscled area to the upper part of the pectoral chest muscles, and down to the forearm.

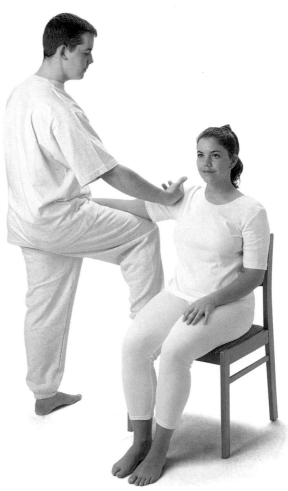

Rolling along the Large Intestine Meridian lifts heaviness and tension in the shoulders, and also eases any pain.

◁ STEP 2   SQUEEZING AND KNEADING THE RIGHT ARM

Grasping the muscle on the top of the shoulder with your right hand, squeeze firmly and knead deeply between your fingers and the heel of your hand. Continue like this down the arm. Repeat this several times and then squeeze with the fingers and thumb lightly all the way down the arm, giving a slight lift between each position. Change hands frequently.

Squeezing and kneading clears the energy channels in the shoulders, loosening the muscles.

STEP 3   PRESSING QI-POINTS

With either hand, press into Qi-points **LI 15** (see
p. 44) and **SJ 14** with your thumb and middle finger.
Press and knead deeply with a rocking motion for at
least 30 seconds, and for several minutes if there is
any shoulder pain. Then knead **LU 1** and **LU 2,**
not too deeply as they can be tender.

LI 15 and *SJ 14* relieve arthritic
pain, stiff joints, and general pain in
the shoulder. Stimulating the Lung
Meridian Qi-points boosts Qi in the
lungs, relieving chest problems, and
colds and flu symptoms.

STEP 4   ROLLING THE TOP OF THE ARM ▷

Facing your partner's side, stand with your foot up
and your knee facing her armpit. Her upper arm is
supported across your knee with the forearm bent.
Use the double BODYHARMONICS® roll up the deltoid
muscle to the border of the shoulder bone, but not
over it. Roll for several minutes.

*Rolling deeply here is very effective in
easing pain and heaviness, particularly
when* **LI 15** *and* **SJ 14** *are
stimulated strongly.*

STEP 5   SQUEEZING AND KNEADING THE TOP ARM

Repeat the squeezing and kneading of Step 2 on the upper
arm only. Use your right hand to squeeze and push backward
up the muscles of the arm, and your left hand to squeeze
and push forward.

STEP 6   PRESSING QI-POINTS
Repeat Step 3.

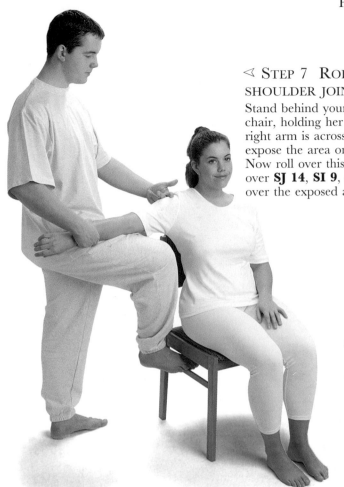

◁ STEP 7 ROLLING THE BACK OF THE SHOULDER JOINT

Stand behind your partner, with one foot on the chair, holding her wrist with your right hand so her right arm is across your knee. Turn the arm to expose the area on the back of the shoulder joint. Now roll over this area with your left hand. Roll over **SJ 14**, **SI 9**, and **SI 10** and then roll down over the exposed area of the forearm.

STEP 8 SQUEEZING AND KNEADING THE UPPER ARM

Repeat Step 5 using your left hand, working along the length of the arm firmly and gently, but this time with a forward pushing action.

STEP 9 PRESSING QI-POINTS

Repeat Step 3, pressing and kneading **SJ 14** and **LI 15**, but this time with the thumb pressing into **SJ 14** and the middle finger pressing **LI 15**.

MAIN QI-POINTS
These are found on the Bladder Meridian (shown in blue), Sanjiao Meridian (red), Lung Meridian (white), and Small Intestine Meridian (red).

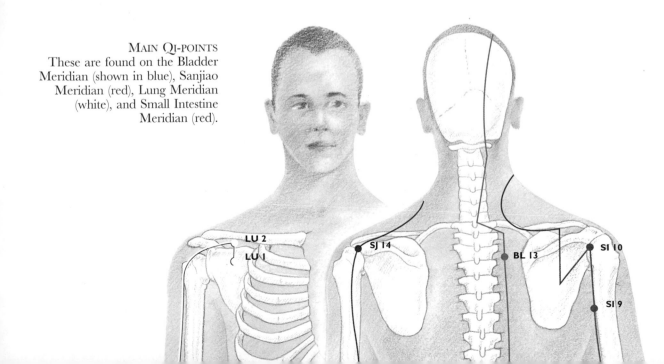

LU 2

LU 1

SJ 14

BL 13

SI 10

SI 9

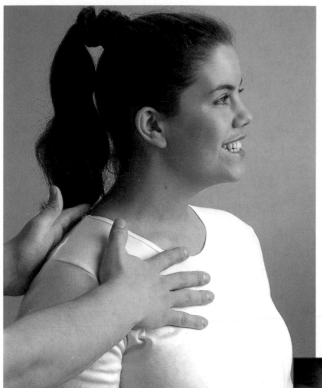

◁ STEP 10 RUBBING THE CHEST AND
SHOULDER BLADES

Put your partner's arm on her lap and stand
facing her right shoulder. Place your right hand
on the right upper area of her chest and your
left hand on her right shoulder blade, wrists
and fingers relaxed. Palmar rub this area with
brisk, light, up and down movements for at
least 30 seconds.

 *This technique stimulates the starting
point of the Lung Meridian and the
Lung point on the back, **BL 13**. It
gives a pleasant sensation and is good
for asthma sufferers and those with
coughs and other chest problems.*

STEP 11 INTERLOCKED HAND ▷
SQUEEZE AND KNEAD

Place your hands across the top of your
partner's right shoulder, with fingers
interlocked. The heels of your hands tuck tightly
into the hollows on the back and front of the
shoulder – you may need to loosen your fingers
to do this. Then knead deeply with the heels of
both hands, making circular movements, for
about 20 seconds.

 *This technique increases blood flow
and improves shoulder mobility; it
should always be used on a
"frozen shoulder".*

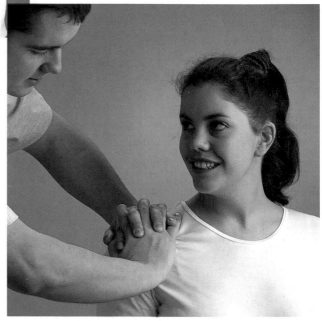

▽ STEP 12 RUBBING DOWN THE ARM

Support your partner's arm between your hands, just below the armpit. The arm should be completely relaxed. Using the palms in opposition technique, rub rapidly to and fro, massaging the arm muscles down to the wrist.

This technique powerfully stimulates the flow of Qi in all the Meridians of the arm.

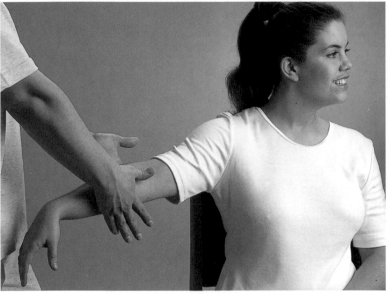

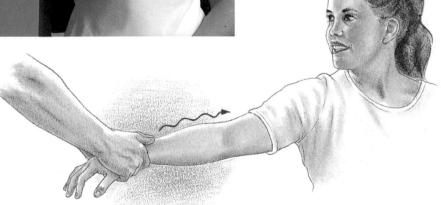

STEP 13 SHAKING THE ARM △

Hold your partner's hand firmly with both your hands, your thumbs together on the top of the wrist. Raise her arm to just below the horizontal and pull gently to loosen the shoulder joint. Then shake 20–30 times with small up and down movements.

This technique greatly relieves shoulder stiffness, as well as pain in the arm and shoulder area, and the side of the neck. When Qi balance is established in the neck, shoulders, and arms, you can feel like a completely new person.

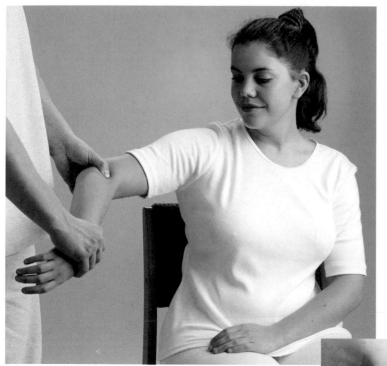

◁ STEP 14 PRESSING AND KNEADING ARM QI-POINTS

Press and knead **LI 11** and **H 3** with the thumb and middle finger. At the same time rotate the forearm with your other hand, holding the wrist lightly. Press and knead **LU 5** and **LU 6**, then press and knead **SJ 5** and **P 6** together, using your thumb and middle finger like pincers.

LI 11 and H 3 treat elbow pain. LU 5 and LU 6 boost Lung energy and help asthmatics. P 6 and SJ 5 have a powerful calming effect on the mind and emotions.

STEP 15 PRESSING AND KNEADING ▷ HAND AND WRIST

Hold the wrist with both your thumbs on top and use your middle fingers under the palm to flick the hand upward several times, allowing the hand to drop under its own weight each time. Then press and knead points **LU 7**, **LU 9**, and **LU 10**.

This step stimulates the Sanjiao, the Pericardium, and the Lung Meridians, which pass through the wrist, and also eases numbness in the thumb and 3rd and 4th fingers.

STEP 16 HAND STRETCH ▷

With your partner's palm facing down, grip the sides of his hand between your fingers and the heel of your thumb. Stretch the hand sideways, several times. Turn the hand so the palm is upward and repeat the technique. Then press and knead **P 8**.

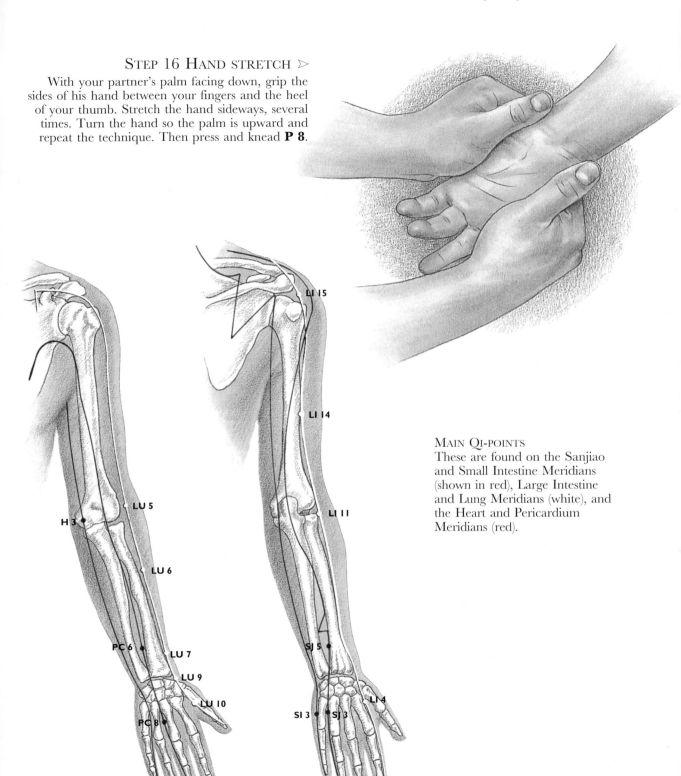

MAIN QI-POINTS
These are found on the Sanjiao and Small Intestine Meridians (shown in red), Large Intestine and Lung Meridians (white), and the Heart and Pericardium Meridians (red).

LI 15

LI 14

LI 11

LU 5

H 3

LU 6

PC 6   LU 7

LU 9

LU 10

PC 8

SJ 5

SI 3   SJ 3   LI 4

▽ STEP 17   ROTATING WRIST, FINGERS, AND THUMB

With your left hand grasp the forearm just above the wrist, and with your right hand grasp the fingers. Rotate the hand on the wrist in both directions.

This unblocks energy at the wrist points of all six Meridians passing through the wrist.

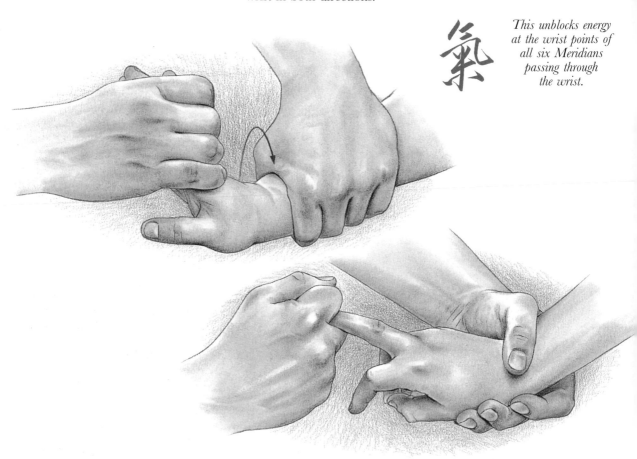

STEP 18   PULLING THE FINGERS △

Still supporting the wrist with your left hand, rotate each of the thumb and fingers in turn. Then pull each one smartly by grasping the base of each digit between your crooked index and second fingers. Finally roll each finger and thumb in turn firmly between your palms.

Each pull exerts a stretch on the wrist. The technique also stimulates all the six Meridians which begin or end in the fingers (see p. 19).

STEP 19 PRESSING AND KNEADING THE JOINTS ▽

Using your index finger and thumb, firmly press and knead all the finger joints and knuckles in turn. Then press and knead **LI 4**, **SJ 3**, and **SI 3**.
Caution: do not use **LI 4** during pregnancy.

Hand and wrist massage presses some of the most powerful Qi-points, increasing the overall feeling of wellbeing.

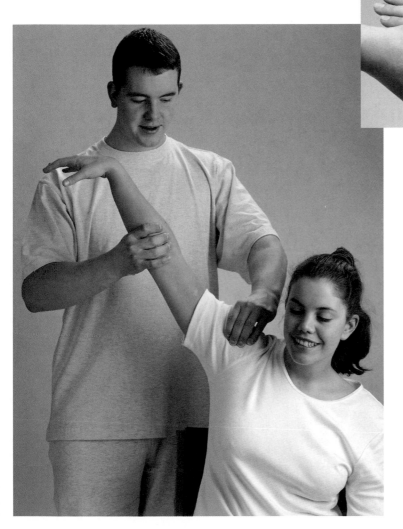

◁ STEP 20 ROTATING THE ARM

Stand behind your partner's right shoulder. With your left hand, grasp the top of the shoulder with your thumb over **SJ 14** and your middle finger over **LI 15**. Support her right arm with your right hand under her elbow. Gently rotate the arm backward with small movements, gradually increasing these until you feel resistance. Do not attempt full rotation if there is any pain. Rotate the arm at least 10 times against the pressure of your thumb on **SJ 14**.

The rotation and pressure on Qi-points loosens stiff and painful joints. Those with mobile joints will also enjoy it.

Shoulder, arm, and hand

The sequence starts on the left of the body;
steps for the right follow on page 96.

STEP 1   ROLLING THE BACK OF THE ▷
SHOULDER AND ARM

Stand slightly behind and to the left side of your
partner, facing the same way, and with your right
foot on the chair. Use single hand rolling (either
technique) on the back of the left shoulder with
your right hand. Use your left hand to support the
arm at the wrist, giving it a slight forward twist.

▽ STEP 2   SQUEEZING AND KNEADING
THE BACK OF THE ARM

Grasp the left shoulder muscle, squeezing it firmly
between the fingers and the heel of the hand, and
pushing forward across it. Continue squeezing and
kneading right down the arm. Repeat with a lighter
squeeze. This is important for removing tension.

STEP 3   PRESSING QI-POINTS

Apply firm pressure to **SJ 14** and **LI 15** with
the thumb and middle finger, as in Step 3 on
page 86.

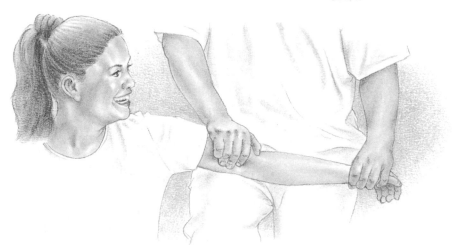

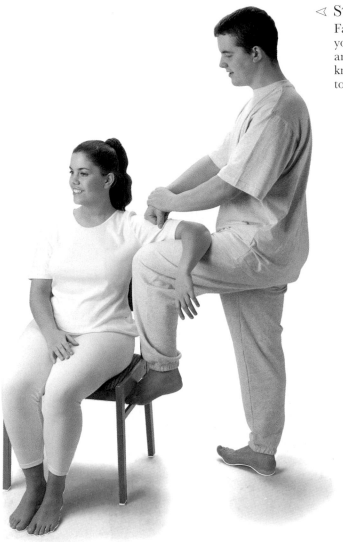

◁ STEP 4 ROLLING THE TOP OF THE ARM
Facing your partner's left shoulder, stand with
your left foot on the chair and support her left
arm, with the forearm bent, on your right
knee. Use the BODYHARMONICS® roll along the
top of the deltoid muscle.

STEP 5 SQUEEZING AND KNEADING
THE TOP OF THE ARM
Repeat the squeezing and kneading action
of Step 2 across the shoulder muscle and
upper arm. Use your right hand to squeeze
and push forward, and your left hand to
squeeze and push backward.

STEP 6 PRESSING QI-POINTS
Press and knead points **LI 15** and
SJ 14 as in Step 3.

◁ STEP 7 ROLLING THE FRONT OF
THE LEFT SHOULDER JOINT
Stand facing your partner's left side with
your foot on the chair. Support her left arm
with your right hand around the wrist,
turning it back slightly to expose the front
of the shoulder. Roll (either technique) over
this area with your left hand up to the
upper part of the pectoral muscles and
down to the forearm. Continue for at least
one minute, and for longer if there is pain
in this area.

STEP 8
Repeat the squeezing and kneading of Step 2 along the whole
arm, this time pushing firmly backward. Also repeat the light
squeezing up and down the arm.

STEP 9
Repeat Step 3, pressing **L1 15** and **SJ 14** again.

STEPS 10–20
REPEAT STEPS 10–20 FROM PAGES 88–93,
THIS TIME ON THE LEFT OF THE BODY.

When you have finished both arms and shoulders,
return to the neck and shoulders and repeat any of
the steps to leave your partner feeling totally relaxed.

*The routine described so far is for
balancing the Qi and will leave your
partner invigorated, relaxed, and
sparkling.*

STEP 21 LEVERED UPPER BACK STRETCH ▷

Your partner raises her arms and with fingers interlocked, turns her palms upward above her head. Stand behind her and place the palm of your right hand in the middle of her upper back (over thoracic vertebrae 5 and 6), fingers toward the neck. Grasp her joined hands with your left hand and gently pull them toward you while pushing forward with your right hand. Be very sensitive and do not pull the hands back farther than is comfortable for her.

Caution: do not attempt this or Step 22 with an elderly or frail partner.

This shoulder manipulation is one of the most effective ways of releasing some of the layers of tension that so often accumulate across the shoulders.

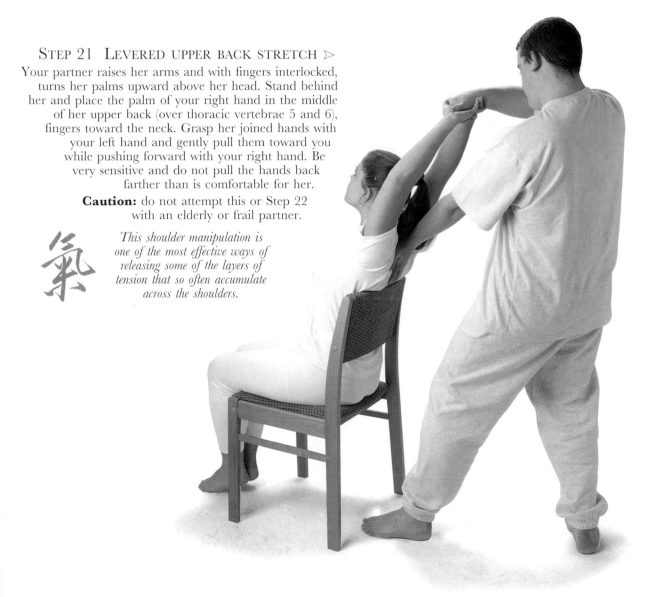

STEP 22 SHOULDER STRETCH ▷

Standing behind your partner, with her arms raised above her head, grasp each hand under the wrist on the thumb side. Draw her arms apart and back until you feel resistance. Ask your partner to relax. Hold the position for at least 15 seconds.

Like Step 21, this manipulation gives a wonderful stretch to the front of the shoulders while relaxing the muscles between the shoulder blades. It also stretches the pectoral muscles.

◁ STEP 23 DEEP STROKING AND PUMMELLING ON THE BACK

Your partner sits on the edge of the chair with legs straight, leaning forward to touch her legs as far down as possible. Make at least five deep palmar strokes down either side of the spine to the lumbar region. Also push forcefully down the spine several times. Then pummel down both sides of the spine (not *on* the spine) alternating your hands, starting at the top.

This technique loosens the lower back, balances Qi in the Bladder and Du Meridians, and leaves your partner very relaxed but invigorated. It is a good way to finish the sitting routine.

PART THREE

Back and hip

Your partner lies face down, his arms by his sides. This part of the routine stimulates the *Shu* points of the back (see page 24), reduces tension in the upper back, and relieves lower back pain and sciatica. Steps 1–7 work on the left side; steps for the right follow on page 101.

STEP 1   PRESSING WITH ROCKING ▷

Stand on your partner's left side. Place your right hand lightly across the sacrum and gradually push the hips into a rocking motion from side to side. Now place your left hand between the shoulder blades, the heel of the hand pressing on the tissues beside the spine on your side. Keeping up the hip rocking motion, push and press toward the spine with your left hand, working slowly down the back to the lumbar area. Starting from the shoulder blade area again, repeat with the left hand down the other side of the spine, pushing and pressing away from the spine. Do not press directly on the spine. Repeat this pressing up to 10 times.

This gentle pressure with rocking motion awakens the sleeping Qi, relaxing the whole body and preparing it for the much deeper stimulation to come.

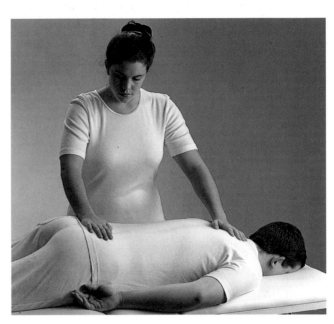

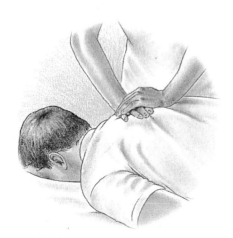

◁ STEP 2   DOUBLE HAND KNEADING

Place the heels of both hands side by side between the spine and the left shoulder blade, level with **BL 13**. Cross the fingers of the left hand over those of the right. With a circular motion, knead vigorously in one place about 20 times until you see the movement in the whole body. Then work in this way down the back to the sacrum. Repeat several times.

The kneading promotes the flow of Qi in the inner and outer Bladder Meridian which is very invigorating.

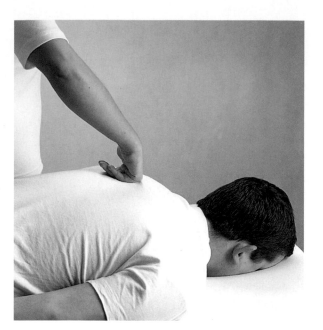

◁ Step 3 Rolling down the back

Stand beside your partner, facing toward his head. Place your right hand between the spine and left shoulder blade, level with thoracic vertebra 2. Use the BODYHARMONICS® roll down the left of the spine to the sacrum. Lift your hand rather than sliding it between positions, and roll about 30 times in each position.

This technique stimulates the inner Bladder Meridian. The rhythm aids relaxation and softens knotted muscles. Rolling also enhances Qi-flow.

◁ Step 4 Rolling toward the spine

Facing your partner, use the double BODYHARMONICS® roll progressing from the top of the back down to the lumbar area. Roll toward the spine, at least 20 times at each position. During each roll your knuckles are over the spinous processes, but do not put any weight on them.

The combined effects of these rolling techniques on the Bladder Meridian release tension throughout the back.

Step 5 Plucking along the spine ▷

Pluck toward the spine, following the same path as Step 4. Be guided by your partner in how much pressure to use, increasing the pressure on the lower back.

This series of techniques increases Qi-flow through the back and all the Organs affected by the Bladder Meridian.

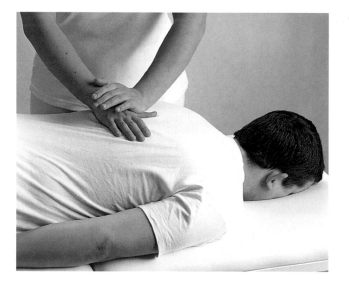

STEP 6 SQUEEZING AND KNEADING ▷ QI-POINTS

With the middle finger and thumb of the right hand on top of the the middle finger and thumb of the left, press the **BL 23** points on both sides of the spine simultaneously. Start kneading lightly to relax the muscle, then increase the pressure and the size of movement, setting up a body rocking action from the wrist. Repeat on **BL 25**. Your partner may well feel "pleasurable pain" with this technique.

BL 23 and BL 25 have a key role in maintaining Qi balance in the lumbar area. BL 23 stimulates the Kidney which stores essential Qi. Massaging BL 25 can also relieve constipation and diarrhoea.

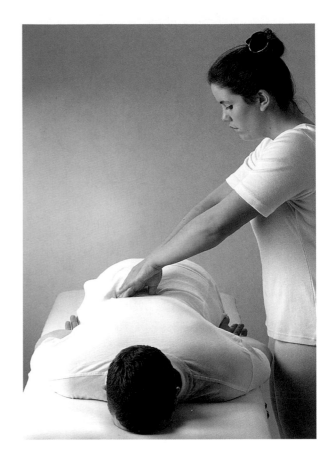

◁ STEP 7 CHINESE ROLLING ON THE BACK

Using either hand or alternating hands, Chinese roll lightly and quickly all over the back. Do not make more than one or two rolls on any point.

This relaxing technique contrasts sharply with the previous more penetrating and uncomfortable ones. Any residual tension is dispersed, leaving your partner feeling relaxed and ready for the next phase.

REPEAT STEPS 1–7 ON YOUR PARTNER'S RIGHT SIDE

In Step 3 face your partner's feet and not his head when rolling down the side of the spine, to ensure that you use your stronger hand.

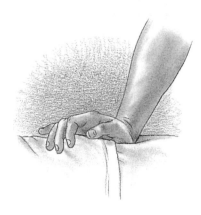

◁ STEP 8 BUTTOCK PRESSING
AND KNEADING

Standing on your partner's right, knead and squeeze with one or both hands over the right buttock muscle, pushing toward the sacrum. Forearm knead over the whole area to relax the muscles, then apply more pressure gradually, pressing and kneading with the thumb or heel of the hand. Finally press and knead **GB 30** and **BL 54** with the elbow, making small circular movements. Lean in gradually with your body weight to give more pressure. Move to the other side and repeat on the left buttock.

 The Qi-points in this step are "gateway points" through which Qi flows between the spine and the legs. This Qi-generating massage sequence is vital for lower back flexibility; it relieves chronic back pain, and is wonderful for sciatica sufferers.

STEP 9 PERCUSSION ON THE BACK ▷
AND BUTTOCKS

Stand on your partner's left and use cupping over the buttocks and sacrum. Then cup up the spine with the hand lengthways along it. Use some force over the buttocks and sacrum but go gently along the spine. Repeat three times. Then, still standing on your partner's left, pummel quickly, lightly, and rhythmically several times down both sides of the spine, *not* on the spine itself. Finish with hacking on all areas of soft tissue on the back.

 These percussive techniques are tremendously stimulating and leave your partner feeling very light; they stimulate the circulation and lymph drainage.

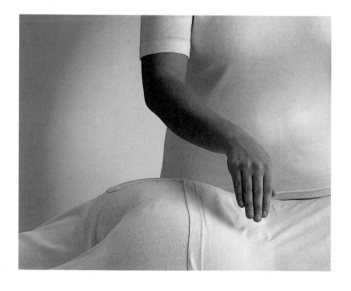

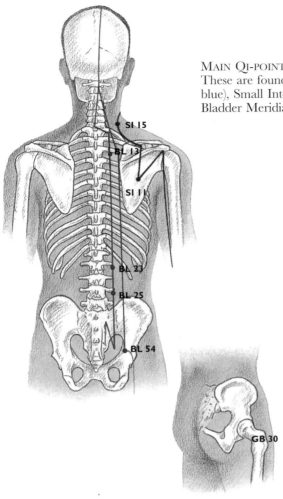

Main Qi-points for back and hip massage
These are found on the Bladder Meridian (shown in blue), Small Intestine Meridian (red), and Gall Bladder Meridian (green).

STEP 10 KNEADING QI-POINTS

Knead all the Bladder Meridian Qi-points in turn, from **BL 11** to **BL 23** (see p. 48). Use either thumb kneading on both sides of the spine simultaneously, or elbow kneading down one side at a time. Also knead **SI 11** and **SI 15**.

The Bladder Meridian Shu points influence the functions of specific Organs (see p. 24). This part of the routine promotes a feeling of energetic, relaxed wellbeing.

STEP 11 SHOULDER ROTATION ▷

Standing on your partner's left, lift and bend his right arm behind him, resting the forearm across the middle of his back. Lean over and slide your right hand under his elbow and up to the shoulder, and grasp it firmly. Your partner's elbow should lie on top of your forearm. Grasping the top of the shoulder with your left hand, rotate it slowly several times, starting with small movements and gradually making larger rotations.

This technique greatly facilitates Qi-flow through the shoulders and into the arms, improving shoulder mobility.

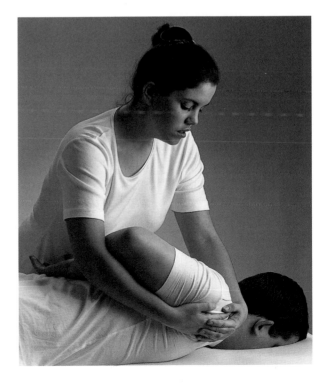

STEP 12   SHOULDER PULL WITH ▷ SCAPULAR PRESS

Retain your grip on the shoulder with your right hand, from Step 11. Slide your left hand down the back so your thumb is pressed against the lower edge of the scapula with the index finger snug on its inner edge. Lift the shoulder, while pressing deeply toward the bone edges around the inner and lower borders of the scapula.

This relaxes the rhomboid muscles between the spine and scapula, easing tension in the upper body.

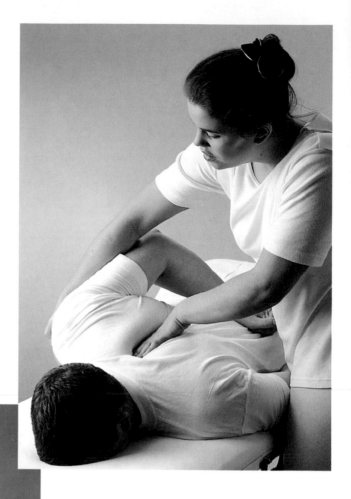

◁ STEP 13   SHOULDER PULL WITH LUMBAR PUSH

Stand facing your partner's left side. Grasp his right shoulder with your left hand. Press down firmly with the palm of your right hand on the lower lumbar area on the side of the spine nearest you. Lean backward to lift his shoulder up while you apply an equal and opposite force to the lower back.

This powerful stretch aids mobility of the shoulder joint and helps relieve fibrositis and bursitis. The twisting action also benefits the thoracic spine.

REPEAT STEPS 11–13 ON THE OTHER SIDE OF THE BODY.

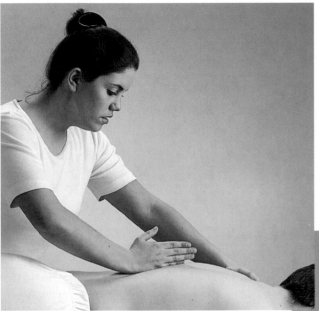

◁ STEP 14 CHAFING THE BACK

This is best done on a bare back, using a little massage oil on the skin. Standing on your partner's left, chafe rapidly along each side of the spine in turn. Use long, firm strokes, at least 20 strokes on each side. Then use two-hand chafing across the sacrum, making at least 50 very rapid, short strokes.

 Chafing stimulates the Bladder Meridian and the Kidneys. On the sacrum it can bring warmth down to the feet because it moves Qi rapidly through the Meridians in the legs.

STEP 15 FOREARM RUBBING ON ▷ THE BACK

Start with your forearms together across the middle of the back. Move your arms apart as you rub over the entire back, leaning in with your body weight to apply deep pressure. Then work from your partner's right side to stimulate the other side of the back equally.

 This technique gently stretches the back, helping to relax muscles deeply.

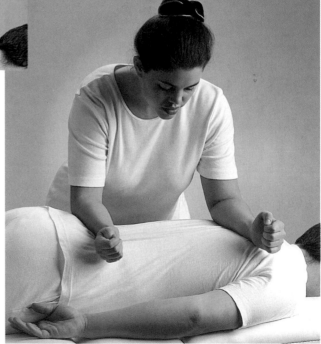

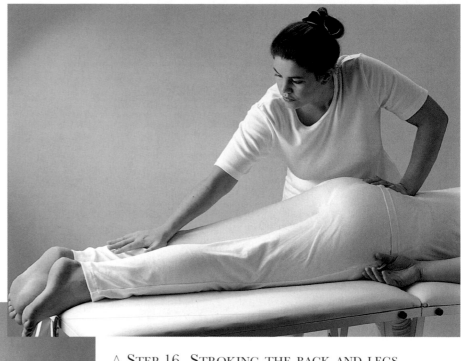

△ STEP 16 STROKING THE BACK AND LEGS

Standing on your partner's left side, place your right hand along the spine at the base of the neck, fingers pointing toward the feet. Stroke firmly, with a deep pushing action, down the midline to the sacrum. Then start at shoulder level and stroke down each side of the spine, over the buttocks, and down each leg. On each ankle squeeze deeply with middle finger and thumb into **BL 60** (p. 49) and **K 3** (p. 46).

Stroking in this way helps the body assimilate the massage. It assists the flow of Qi down the Bladder Meridian and balances Kidney yin and Bladder yang, giving a remarkably grounded and deeply relaxed feeling.

△ STEP 17 RUBBING THE BACK

Rub with your right palm, making large circular movements over the entire surface of the back between the base of the neck and the sacrum. Then use both hands to rub with a loose, light, side-to-side action from the wrist, hands moving in opposite directions. Start at the shoulders, progressing down the back, over the buttocks, and the backs of the legs to the ankles. Keep the action rapid and repeat as many times as you like.

These rubbing techniques have a wonderfully calming effect by restoring the natural flow of Qi.

PART FOUR

Back of leg and foot

Carry out Steps 1–8 on one leg first, then
repeat them on the other leg.

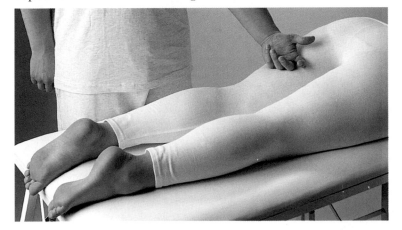

◁ STEP 1   ROLLING THE LEG

With your partner lying face down,
stand beside her and use Chinese or
BODYHARMONICS® rolling on the leg
nearest to you. Work from the base
of the buttock down to the ankle.
Repeat at least twice.

STEP 2   KNEADING THE LEG ▷

Knead deeply across the leg with the heel of
one hand, starting just below the buttocks
and working down to the ankle. Repeat the
kneading using both hands.

STEP 3   SQUEEZING THE LEG ▷

Start with a light, whole hand squeeze. With your
thumb on one side of the leg and fingers on the
other, keep up an even pressure as you squeeze
gently down the leg. Repeat this light squeezing five
times or more. Then, using both hands side by side
and deeper pressure, squeeze up and down the
length of the leg several times.

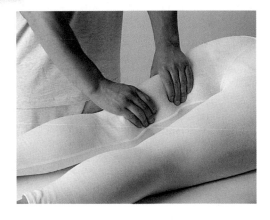

MAIN QI-POINTS FOR BACK OF
LEG AND FOOT
These are found on the Bladder
Meridian (shown in blue), Kidney
Meridian (blue), and Gall Bladder
Meridian (green).

STEP 4 PRESSING AND KNEADING QI-POINTS

Press deeply with the thumb or
elbow, using a rotary kneading
action, into **BL 36**, **BL 37**, **BL
40**, and **BL 57**. Apply pressure
gently and increase gradually,
being sensitive to your partner.
Knead **BL 60** and **K 3** together
with middle finger and thumb.

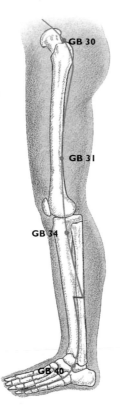

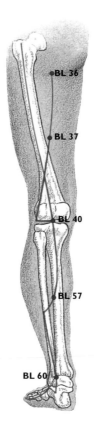

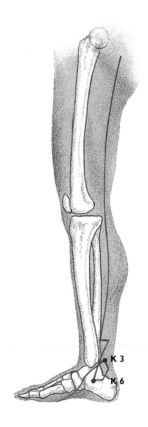

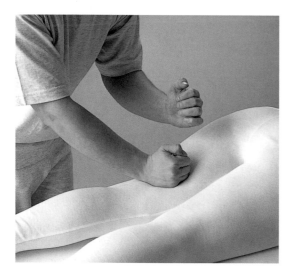

◁ STEP 5 PERCUSSION ON THE LEGS

Use hacking with two hands, or pummelling, or both.
Work from just below the buttocks down the middle of
the back of the legs, and down the outer margin. Repeat
up and down the back of each leg two or three times.
You can also use one-handed cupping.

*These treatments leave the legs feeling
wonderfully light. They relax tense and
sore muscles and tendons, and relieve some
types of sciatica and lower back pain.*

STEP 6 LEG IN FROG POSITION ▷

Lift one leg slightly, bend the knee and push it out to the side. Place the foot across the back of the other knee. Use rolling, kneading, squeezing, and percussion on the bent leg, and press and knead **GB 30**, **GB 31**, and **GB 34**.

*This step works on the Gall Bladder Meridian, powerfully affecting sciatica. **GB 34** is the main point for relieving muscle and tendon problems all over the body.*

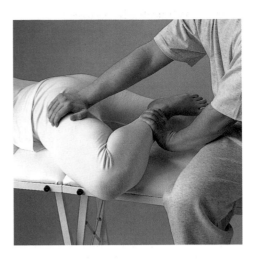

◁ STEP 7 HIP ROTATION, AND LEG LIFT WITH LUMBAR PRESS

Place one hand over **BL 25** on the side of the spine nearest you. Press there while you lift the straight leg, supporting it just above the knee on your other forearm. Raise the leg until you feel resistance and then rotate it in small circles. Pause a moment, then lift the leg higher, pressing down on the lumbar area. Hold for several seconds before lowering the leg.

These manipulations increase mobility in hips and knees. They effectively treat slipped lumbar discs, sciatica, and lower back pain.

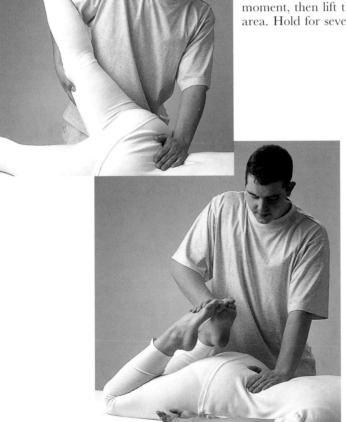

◁ STEP 8 LUMBAR PRESS WITH FLEXED LEGS

Place one hand on the sacrum with its outer edge just touching the lumbar area. Bend both your partner's legs toward the buttocks with your hand across the top of her ankles. Press her feet while pressing deeply on the back for 10 seconds.

This manipulation treats lower back and ilio-sacral pain, and stimulates Qi-flow through the pelvic area.

REPEAT STEPS 1–8 ON
THE OTHER LEG

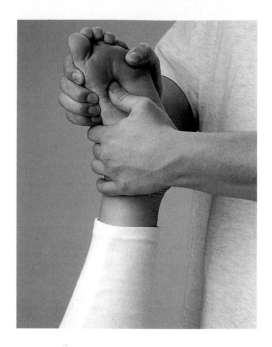

Follow Steps 9–13 on one foot, and then repeat on the other.

STEP 9 THUMB KNEADING AND PUMMELLING ▷

With your partner lying face down, lift the lower leg nearest to you to expose the sole of the foot. Supporting the top of the foot with one hand, use the thumb of the other to knead deeply, all over the sole. Then pummel all over the sole using the edge of your lightly clenched fist.

STEP 10 FOOT ROTATION ▷

Grasp around the back of the ankle, pressing into **GB 40** and **K 6** with the thumb and middle finger. Holding the toes with your other hand, rotate the foot in as near a circle as you can. Repeat the rotation in the opposite direction.

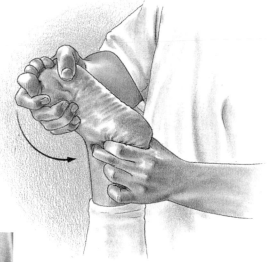

Six Meridians pass through the ankles. These techniques stimulate Qi-flow through them very effectively.

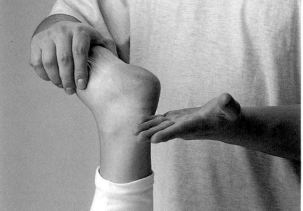

◁ STEP 11 HACKING THE ACHILLES TENDON

Support the front of the foot, pressing down on the toes to stretch the Achilles tendon. Slightly spread the fingers of the other hand and gently hack the tendon with the little finger.

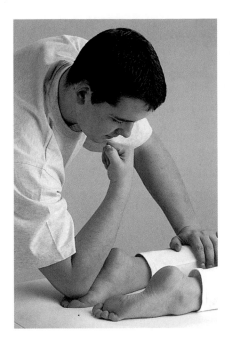

◁ STEP 12 FOOT KNEADING AND PUMMELLING
Lower the foot and knead the sole deeply, using either the thumb
or the elbow. Knead into **K 1** (p. 46) for at least 30 seconds.
Then pummel the sole of the foot vigorously.

STEP 13 CHAFING THE SOLE ▷
Holding the lower leg, chafe vigorously on the sole of
the foot, following a diagonal line over **K 1**.
Chafe for at least 30 seconds.

*Feet always respond well to massage. Tui
Na on the sole over **K 1** brings the Qi
downward giving a wonderfully
grounded feeling.*

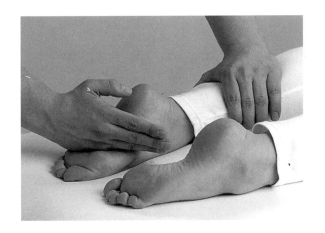

REPEAT STEPS 9–13 ON THE OTHER FOOT

STEP 14 LATERAL LEG SWING ▷
Grasp both feet under the ankles and lift them a
little. Lean backward, pulling the legs gently and
then swing them together from side to side
creating a gentle rock on the hips and spine.
Swing for at least 20 seconds.

*This manipulation loosens the hip joints
and relaxes the spinal muscles.*

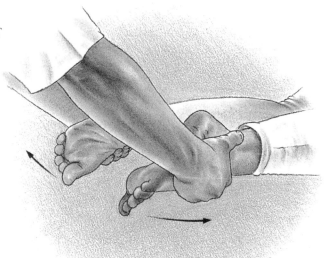

PART FIVE
Lower back, hip, and leg

Carry out Steps 1 and 2 first on one side
then the other.

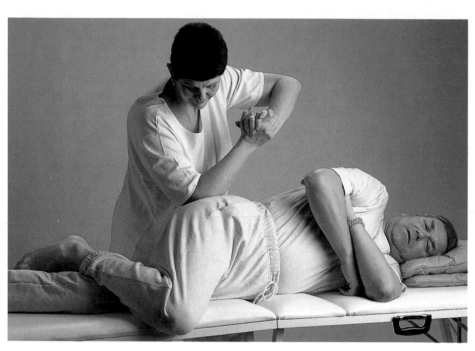

△ STEP 1 PRESSING AND KNEADING QI-POINTS

Your partner lies on his left side with a small pillow supporting his head. The left
leg is straight. Bend his right leg and draw it up in front so the thigh is at right
angles to the body. Standing behind your partner and leaning over the right hip,
or sitting beside his abdomen, elbow knead **GB 30** for at least two minutes with
small, circular movements. Start lightly and gradually put more body weight
behind it. Then squeeze with the whole hand, and knead with the heel of the
hand, down the bent leg. Press and knead **GB 31**.

*Deep kneading of **GB 30** can be uncomfortable
but strongly relieves sciatica, however severe.*

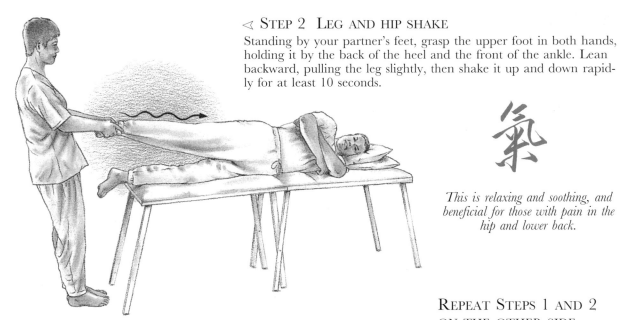

◁ STEP 2 LEG AND HIP SHAKE

Standing by your partner's feet, grasp the upper foot in both hands, holding it by the back of the heel and the front of the ankle. Lean backward, pulling the leg slightly, then shake it up and down rapidly for at least 10 seconds.

This is relaxing and soothing, and beneficial for those with pain in the hip and lower back.

REPEAT STEPS 1 AND 2 ON THE OTHER SIDE

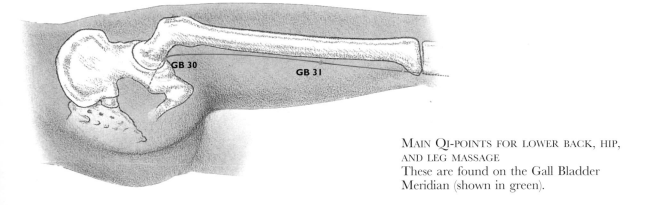

MAIN QI-POINTS FOR LOWER BACK, HIP, AND LEG MASSAGE
These are found on the Gall Bladder Meridian (shown in green).

PART SIX

Front of leg and foot

Carry out Steps 1–8 first on one leg and then on the other.

STEP 1 FRONT OF THE LEG ▷

With your partner lying on her back, repeat Steps 1, 2, 3, and 5 from Part Four, pages 107–8: rolling, kneading, squeezing (see right), and percussion. Press and knead **ST 31**, **ST 34**, **ST 36**, and **ST 40**.

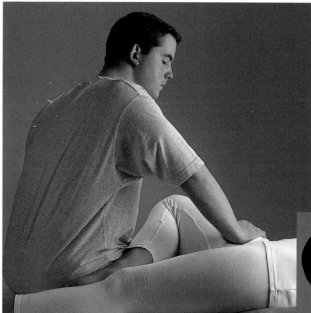

◁ **STEP 2 INSIDE THE BENT LEG**

Bend the leg out to the side, keeping the foot tucked against the straight leg. Palm press, then knead and squeeze all along the inside of the bent leg. Thumb press and knead **SP 6, SP 9,** and **SP 10**.

Caution: do not use **SP 6** during pregnancy.

Step 1 improves hip and leg mobility, kidney and bowel function, and relieves chesty cough and phlegm. Step 2 is good for PMT, and genital problems, swelling, insomnia, worry, and skin troubles.

STEP 3 PRESSING THE CALF ▷

Line up the foot of the bent leg with the knee of the straight leg and lift the knee upright. Sitting on the toes of the bent leg, place both hands behind the calf muscle and press them toward you. Knead **BL 57** (see p. 49) with your fingers.

Deep pressure on the calf muscles relieves tension, spasm, and sciatic pain in the lower leg.

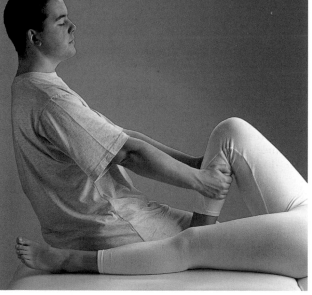

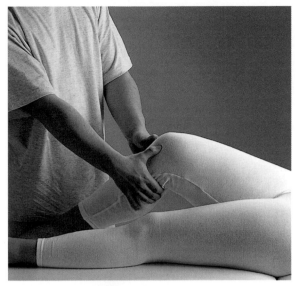

◁ STEP 4   KNEE PRESSING WITH EXTENSION
With the leg straight, find the two depressions just
below the kneecap. **ST 35** is in the outside one.
Supporting the leg with your fingers under the upper
calf, press your thumb-tips into each depression.
Then lift the knee up about one foot (30 cm). Press
deeply into the depressions again and pull the leg
slightly toward you. Repeat this action several times.

*These techniques relieve knee pain and
improve mobility.*

MAIN QI-POINTS FOR FRONT OF LEG AND FOOT MASSAGE
These are found on the Stomach Meridian (shown in
yellow), the Liver Meridian (green), Kidney Meridian (blue),
and Spleen Meridian (yellow).

△ STEP 5   HIP ROTATION
Lift your partner's lower right leg over
your forearm and support the top of
her knee with both hands, fingers
inter-locked. Lean forward and rotate
the thigh using small, circular
movements, increasing to larger
circles, but without causing pain.

*This is excellent treatment for stiff
hip joints, arthritic hips, pain in
the groin area associated with
sciatica, lumbago, and
ilio-sacral pain.*

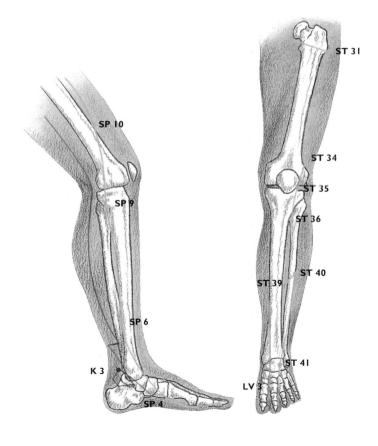

STEP 6 KNEE-HIP ULTRA FLEX ▷

Bend the knee to the chest so the shin is horizontal. Lean on the leg with your body weight, pressing for several seconds with your forearm across the upper shin and your other hand over the ankle. Keeping the leg tightly bent, pummel the buttock area with a lightly clenched fist.

These techniques relieve hamstrings that are tense or in spasm.

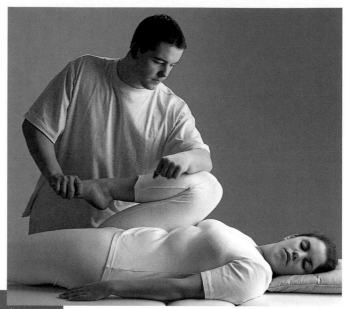

◁ STEP 7 ZIG-ZAG HIP-KNEE ROCK

With the leg bent so the shin is horizontal, hold the knee with one hand and the heel with the other. Without pressure, swing the knee outward while swinging the heel toward the midline. Then reverse the movement to create a to and fro action, giving at least five swings in each direction.

This gives a further boost to hip mobility and also benefits the knee.

Step 8 Knee extension and flexion ▷

Start with the knee bent so that the thigh is vertical and the shin horizontal. Hold the heel in one hand and support the knee with the other. Push the leg gently toward the head, without much pressure. Pause, and then extend it rapidly by pushing on the knee and pulling back on the heel. Repeat this sequence several times.

 Done very gently, this relieves knee pain, especially of the ligaments. It strengthens the lower back and relieves sciatica.

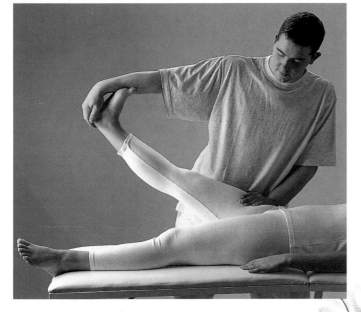

◁ Step 9 Leg and foot stretch

Place one hand under the heel with the sole against your forearm. With your other hand pressing down on the thigh just below the groin, lift the leg keeping it straight. As you raise the leg press your forearm against the foot to create a powerful ankle flexion. Relax and then repeat once or twice.

 This stretch along the Bladder Meridian is excellent for spasm or injury of calf muscles or hamstrings.

Step 10 Single leg shake ▷

Standing at your partner's feet, grasp the heel and ankle with both hands and shake up and down with rapid, small movements.

 This stimulates Qi-flow and relaxes muscles, benefiting the lower back and hip joint.

STEP 11 FOOT ROTATION ▷

Sit on the couch and lift your partner's nearest leg out and across so that her calf rests on your knee. Grasp the ankle with the supporting hand and rotate the foot with the other hand, holding it across the toes.

This aids ankle mobility and should be part of the treatment for ankle pain, sprained ankle, and painful Achilles tendon.

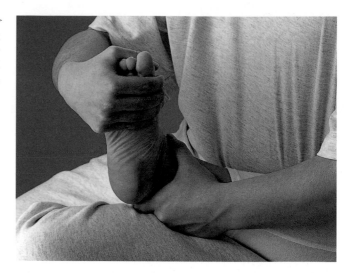

◁ STEP 12 PULLING THE TOES

Grasp each toe in turn between your crooked index and second fingers. Rotate several times, and then pull vigorously.

STEP 13 PRESSING AND KNEADING QI-POINTS ▷

Use thumb pressing and kneading to stimulate **LV 3**, **SP 4**, **ST 41**, **K 3**, **K 6**, and **GB 40**.

These Qi-points on the foot are all effective and important local and distant points. **LV 3**, *for example, directs Qi to the head.*

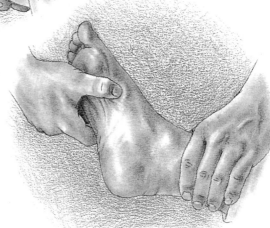

PART SEVEN
Abdomen and chest

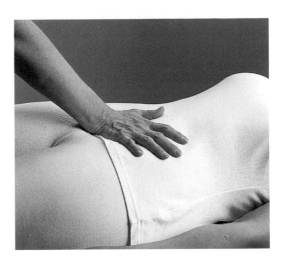

STEP 1 PALMAR RUBBING AND KNEADING ▷

With your partner lying on her back, rub her abdomen just below the navel with your palm using small, clockwise movements. Then knead with the heel of the hand on the centre of the abdomen, gradually increasing the pressure.

Caution: do not massage the abdomen during pregnancy.

These techniques are very relaxing and comforting, stimulating the flow of Qi.

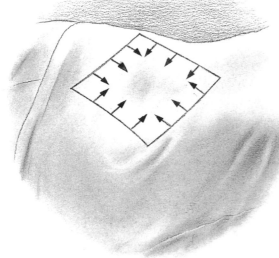

◁ STEP 2 THUMB KNEADING ON ABDOMEN

Start thumb kneading the lower abdomen just above the pubic bone and progress up the right side to just below the ribs and then down again. Repeat for up to five minutes before moving to your partner's other side and thumb kneading in the same way. Use the deepest pressure at waist level.

This technique quite effectively reduces the appetite if done for long enough and with adequate pressure. It also relieves constipation.

STEP 3 INTERLOCKED HAND ▷
SQUEEZE

With fingers interlocked, hand squeeze firmly up and down the centre of the abdomen. Give each squeeze a circular kneading action with the heels of the hands. Repeat this technique for up to two minutes.

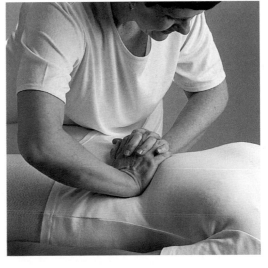

This squeeze relieves menstrual pain and the symptoms of irritable bowel syndrome such as bloatedness and indigestion.

STEP 4 SQUEEZE, LIFT, AND SHAKE ▷

Starting on the far side of the abdomen, squeeze with the fingers and thumbs of both hands as much tissue as you can comfortably hold. Lift it and shake it vigorously several times and then let go. Repeat these actions across the abdomen toward you. If your partner is very overweight, repeat this sequence for up to 10 minutes.

This technique helps to reduce abdominal fat by enhancing the circulation of blood and lymph through the adipose tissue.

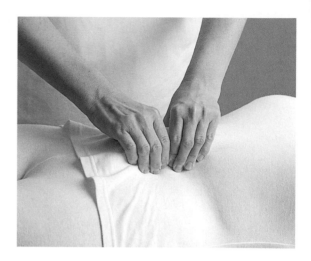

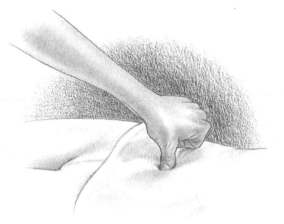

△ STEP 5 THUMB ROCKING

Thumb rock for several minutes on **R 3**, **R 6**, and **R 12**.

All types of sexual, menstrual, and digestive problems can be treated through these Ren points.

MAIN QI-POINTS FOR MASSAGE OF ABDOMEN AND CHEST
These are found on the Lung Meridian (shown in white), the Ren Meridian (black), and the Stomach Meridian (yellow).

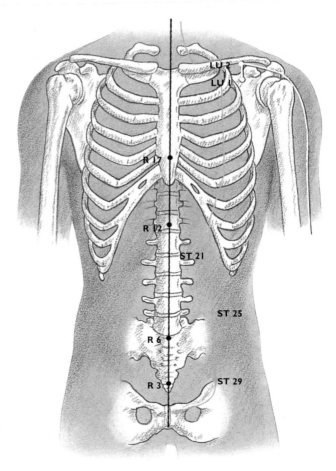

STEP 6 HACKING ON THE ABDOMEN ▷
Using both hands separately, hack lightly over the
entire abdominal area with the fingers loosely apart.

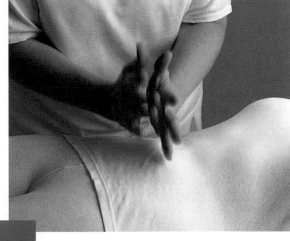

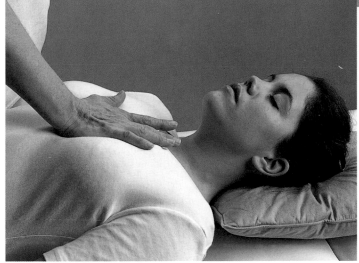

◁ STEP 7 PALMAR RUBBING
THE CHEST
Rub the chest with the palm of one
hand, concentrating on the muscles
between the ribs and the sternum. Press
with the heel of the thumb when rubbing
on the muscles between the ribs.

STEP 8 PRESSING AND KNEADING QI-POINTS
Thumb knead over **R 17**, **LU 1**, and **LU 2**.

*These techniques help relieve asthma
and chest infections.*

PART EIGHT
Face, head, and neck

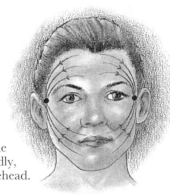

STEP 1   RUBBING AND KNEADING ▷

With your partner lying on her back, stand behind her
head. Use the heels of both thumbs to rub firmly from
the midline of the forehead toward the temples. Then
knead the temples and the sides of the head just above the
ears. Repeat three or four times.

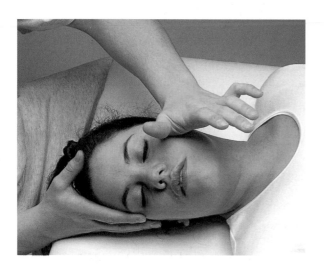

◁ STEP 2   KNEADING THE FACE

Starting in the middle of the forehead, vigorously
knead with the heel of the thumb out toward the
temple, using a rocking action. Continue kneading
back over the forehead to the other temple, at least
three times. Then knead down the cheek area,
round the chin, and up the other cheek.

*These techniques open tissues to the flow
of Qi, stimulating blood circulation
and lymph drainage.*

STEP 3   THUMB STROKING THE FACE ▷

Start with quick, firm thumb strokes from the midline of the
forehead to the **Taiyang** points on the temples (see right). Repeat
several times, moving your starting point from the eyebrows to the
hairline. Then stroke outward to the **Taiyang** points again, from
either side of the nose just below the eyes. Move further down the
cheeks each time, always finishing on the **Taiyang** points.
Next stroke from the chin along the lower jaw. Finally, from the
Yintang point on the forehead between the eyebrows, stroke rapidly,
alternating your thumbs, straight up the centre of the forehead.

STEP 4 THUMB ROCKING ▷

Place the thumb on the **Yintang** point and thumb rock steadily for at least half a minute. Thumb rock along the eyebrow and back round below the eye to the nose, and then on the other eyebrow and eye, following a figure of eight pattern.

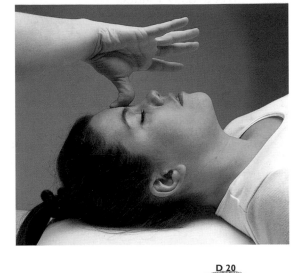

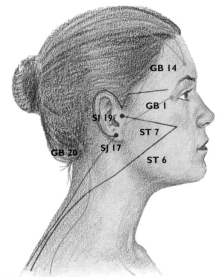

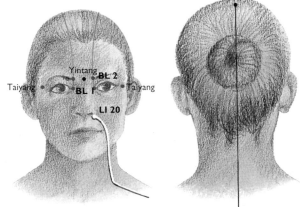

MAIN QI-POINTS FOR FACE, HEAD, AND NECK MASSAGE
These are found on the Bladder Meridian (shown in blue), Small Intestine Meridian (red), Gall Bladder Meridian (green), Sanjiao (red), Stomach Meridian (yellow), and Du (black).

YINTANG
Midway between the inside ends of the eyebrows. Treats insomnia, calms the mind.

TAIYANG
In a depression approximately 1 cun to the side of the outer corner of the eye and eyebrow. Treats all kinds of headaches.

STEP 5 PRESSING AND KNEADING FACE QI-POINTS

Use the index and middle fingers to press and knead **BL 1** and **BL 2** simultaneously at least 20 times, gradually increasing the pressure. Then press and knead with your middle fingers on the **Taiyang** points, **GB 1**, **GB 14**, **ST 6**, and **ST 7**. If your partner suffers from any kind of ear problem, knead **SI 19**, **GB 2**, and **SJ 17**. Knead **LI 20** if there are sinus or other nasal problems.

◁ STEP 6 RUBBING THE HEAD

With your right hand on the left side of your partner's head, rub to and fro around the outer edge of the ear along the Gall Bladder Meridian with the tips of your fingers and thumb. The motion comes from a sideways rocking of the wrist. Repeat with your left hand on the right hand side.

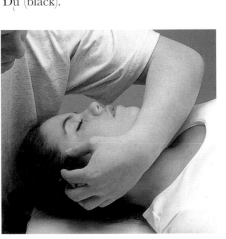

◁ STEP 7 KNEADING THE SCALP
With the fingers of both hands, knead the entire
scalp, using small side-to-side movements.

STEP 8 PRESSING AND KNEADING ▷
QI-POINT
With your thumbs one on top of the other,
press **D 20**. Knead with very small
circular movements for 30 seconds.

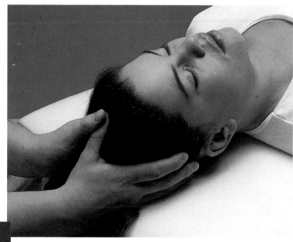

◁ STEP 9 DOUBLE CUPPING
Use both hands held together to double cup
along the forehead and down to the temples.

*The facial massage feels wonderful,
and relieves headaches, sore and
aching eyes, congested sinuses,
toothache, earache, dizziness,
numbness and paralysis of
facial muscles.*

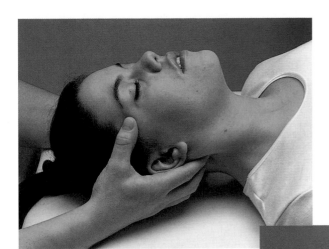

◁ STEP 10 PULLING THE NECK

Slide your hands under the neck to the occipital region of the skull. Your fingers should just meet under the neck. Hook the middle finger of each hand into **GB 20** and pull a little. Sustain the pull and lift for at least one minute.

This technique is excellent treatment for headache and tense, painful neck muscles.

STEP 11 LIFTING THE NECK ▷

Line up the fingers of both your hands under the neck on either side of the spine. With your fingertips, lift first one side and then the other, so that the head rocks from side to side. Repeat several times.

This helps relax tense neck muscles and relieves a stiff neck.

STEP 12 KNEADING THE NECK ▷

Lift the head and turn it gently to one side. Thumb knead with slight pressure along the band of muscle from below the ear toward the collarbone. Press and knead **GB 20**. Repeat on the other side.

This technique is good for side neck tension and pain, and headaches behind the eyes and on the side of the head.

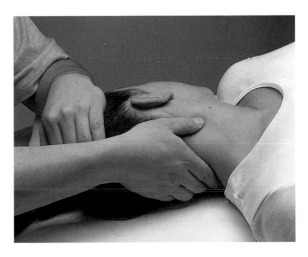

Chapter Six

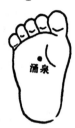

Everyday Tui Na

Once you are familiar with the techniques described in Chapter Four, and have practised giving the whole-body routine in Chapter Five, you will be able to apply that knowledge to relieve everyday symptoms such as headaches and stiff shoulders. The Tui Na treatments in this chapter have been developed for a wide range of ailments and conditions, to tackle the most common underlying causes of the conditions, as well as the symptoms. With the exception of the Tui Na for Infants on page 134, the treatments in this chapter are not suitable for children under the age of five. Before starting any Tui Na treatment, you should check the cautions given on page 12.

One of Tui Na's strengths is in relieving chronic pain: long term, debilitating, but not crippling pain. (*Acute* pain occurs suddenly and is more alarming.) Chronic pain may be caused by "wear and tear" on the joints, often described as arthritis, or by sports or other injuries. Treatments for chronic pain in different parts of the body, or for acute pain

following injury, are presented on pages 128–32. They are listed according to the site of the pain.

The treatments for common ailments on pages 132–4 are arranged alphabetically, by ailment. These include everyday problems such as headache and insomnia, but also the more severe conditions of bronchial asthma and irritable bowel syndrome. These conditions should always be treated by a doctor or trained practitioner, but you can use Tui Na safely to give relief from the symptoms.

Tui Na is a valuable therapy for treating many of the problems associated with different life stages. Treatments particularly suitable for adolescents are described on pages 135–6, and for the elderly on pages 136–7. Three special techniques for babies and infants are given on pages 134–5. These promote health and strengthen the immune system. The chapter ends with a daily self-help routine that will enable you to start every day with your Qi-flow balanced, feeling full of sparkle and vitality.

Underlying causes of pain

Traditional Chinese Medicine regards all pain, whether chronic or acute, as the result of an imbalance in Qi. Balancing Qi-flow can reduce or even eliminate pain, even if the physical problem is "incurable".

Many everyday health problems are caused or exacerbated by stress, which can result from both emotional and physical causes. By identifying the initial causes of tension, you may be able to modify your lifestyle to avoid them. Common physical causes of tension include long periods sitting in a car or at a desk, repetitive physical actions, heavy lifting, gardening, standing for long periods, and sleeping on a soft mattress.

These physical causes of stress are often easy to recognize and in some cases simple to control – by changing your sitting posture, for example. Emotional causes of stress are far more insidious; from the head they create tension in the neck and shoulders, and gradually invade the other body systems. Such stresses often result from interaction with other people, either at work or, at a much deeper level, in personal relationships. They include anger, worry, fear, frustration, grief, and unfulfilled emotions. In the Chinese view, disturbed or excessive emotions are the internal causes that lead to physical problems (see page 11). The external causes include the invasion of the body by the environmental energies such as heat, wind, cold, dryness, and dampness. Other external factors, such as poor diet, lack of exercise, and insufficient sleep, worsen the effects of all these factors.

Treating sports injuries

Exercise and physical activity is vital to maintain health, and sports, games, and fitness training of many kinds are becoming more and more popular. However, along with the recognized health benefits comes the risk of damage to muscles and joints. Tui Na is a highly effective treatment for sports injuries, provided there are no broken bones or ruptured tendons. Torn muscles, or muscles in spasm, bursitis, damaged and inflamed tendons (tenosynovitis), over-stretched ligaments, swelling (oedema), and bruising can all be treated successfully. Begin the treatment as soon after the injury as possible, using direct thumb pressure and kneading on all the Qi-points on and around the site of the injury. Do not massage on newly bruised tissue. Also look for any *ashi* points around the injury – these are tender spots that do not exactly correspond with a Qi-point. Thumb knead any that you find with pressure, as for Qi-points. If the area is badly bruised, or if the skin is broken, treat distant points (see page 22).

The treatments

Each treatment starts with a thorough soft tissue massage to prepare the tissues and joints, using steps from the relevant sections of the whole-body routine in Chapter Five. Once your partner is warm and relaxed, start to work on the Qi-points listed for the treatment, referring to the Meridian illustrations, and the captions that describe the positions of the points, in Chapter Three. Knead deeply on each of these Qi-points for at least three minutes. The most powerfully effective Qi-points for each condition are shown in **bold**, with those used to enhance their effects in *italic*. They are all listed in order of importance. Finish by massaging along the Meridians in that area. For maximum benefit repeat the treatment frequently, until the symptoms subside.

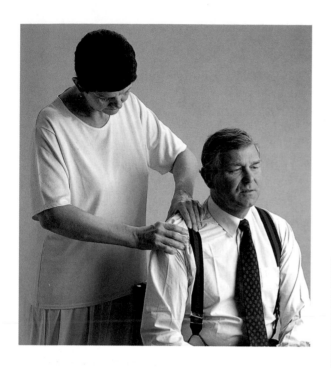

Tui Na on the Large Intestine and Sanjiao
Meridians in the shoulder relieves the shoulder
pain from a skiing injury.

Chronic and acute pain, including sports injuries

For the following, treat the recommended
Qi-points on the side of the body affected.

Neck pain

The muscles in the neck and shoulders store
tension from the arms, the head, and up the
spine, which can lead to chronic pain.
Tension from the arms first becomes notice-
able in the trapezius muscles (see page 138),
with a feeling of heaviness, tightness, and
pain across the shoulders and neck, with
some stiffness.

As tension develops, the muscles shorten
and thicken, becoming knotted and hard.
This tension in the tissues puts pressure on
the nerves, causing pain both locally and
further away in the body, and often resulting
in headache. As tension increases these
changes in the tissues start to block Qi-flow,
resulting in discomfort which can worsen to
severe pain. Even slight tension in this area is
enough to stifle any feeling of relaxation.

Neck pain can also be caused by trauma
such as "whiplash" injuries from accidents or
sports injuries. If there is any degenerative
disease in the cervical spine, sharp sideways
movement can trigger acute pain.

NECK PAIN TREATMENT
Apply Tui Na as described in Chapter
Five, Part 1, Steps 1–7.

General tenseness with or without pain
(the most common condition)
GB 20, BL 10, GB 21

Pain and stiffness down one side
of the neck, possibly radiating down and
causing numbness in the fingers
GB 20, BL 10, GB 21, BL 11
SI 3, SJ 3, SJ 5, LU 7, LI 4, LI 11
Caution: do not use **LI 4** during pregnancy.

Neck tension causing headache
GB 20, BL 10, GB 21
LI 4, LV 3
Caution: do not use **LI 4** during pregnancy.

Sports injury, whiplash
GB 20, BL 10, GB 21
*SI 14, SI 11, SI 12, BL 11, GB 34, LI 4,
LU 7, SI 3*
Caution: do not use **LI 4** during pregnancy.

Lower back pain

Pain in the lumbar area is very common and extremely debilitating. It can be caused by poor posture and standing for long periods. Sitting in poorly designed chairs that do not support the lower back, either driving or at a desk, also creates muscle strain, particularly in the lower back. Acute pain is often triggered by sudden twisting of the waist; lifting heavy loads using the back muscles; heavy digging, and working out in the gym. As we age arthritis may develop in the vertebrae and damage to the discs between them will reduce the mobility of the spine, which can result in severe, chronic pain.

LOWER BACK PAIN TREATMENT
Apply Tui Na as described in Chapter Five, Part 3 with emphasis on Steps 6, 8, and 14; Part 4, Steps 1–5, and Step 7 leg manipulation; and Part 6, Step 10 leg shake.

Chronic pain in lumbar region, often due to "slipped disc" or trapped nerve
BL 23, BL 25
GB 30

Chronic pain in the ilio-sacral region
BL 23, BL 25, GB 30, BL 54
BL 32, BL 40, BL 60

Acute lower back pain due to injury
BL 23, BL 25, GB 30, BL 54
D 4, BL 36, BL 37, BL 40, BL 57, BL 60

Sciatica

Sciatica is chronic pain that radiates from the lower back/sacral region into the legs. It can make walking, sitting, and lying painful. It is frequently difficult to pinpoint the site of sciatic pain, which often seems to permeate the whole leg. While sufferers desperately try to find a comfortable way to stand or walk, they may change their posture, which puts stresses and strains on the spine even up to the neck.

SCIATICA TREATMENT
Apply Tui Na as described in Chapter Five, Part 3, Steps 6 and 8; Part 4, Steps 1–5 and especially Step 6; Part 5, Steps 1–4.

Lower back pain that radiates down one or both legs
BL 25, GB 30, BL 54, GB 31
GB 34, GB 40, BL 36, BL 37, ST 30, ST 31, ST 34

Shoulder pain

Shoulder pain and stiffness have three main causes. The first is degeneration of the ligaments and cartilage in the joint capsule, due to osteo- or rheumatoid arthritis. This is most usual in people over the age of 50. The pain is mostly on the front of the shoulder, and "frozen shoulder" may develop if the sufferer tries to keep it still to avoid pain.

The second cause is bursitis, caused by repetitive strain, perhaps from sport or from carrying heavy shopping. A third major cause of shoulder pain is tension from the arms. Driving for long hours with tense arm muscles but little large-scale movement can have this effect, as can keyboard work.

SHOULDER PAIN TREATMENT
Apply Tui Na as described in Chapter
Five, Part 2, Steps 1–13 and 16.

Pain with or without immobility due to
degenerative condition of the joint
LI 15, SJ 14, LI 14, LI 11

Pain radiating from the scapular area
and/or the back of the armpit
SJ 14, SI 9, SI 10, SI 11, SI 12
LI 15, SI 14, LI 11

Pain in the deltoids and top of the shoulder
LI 15, LI 14, LI 11
SJ 14, LI 4, SI 10, GB 21

Acute pain from soft tissue injury
LI 15, SJ 14, LI 11
SI 9, SI 10, SI 11, SI 12, SI 14 if pain is in
the scapular area
LI 11, LI 14, LI 4 if pain is in the deltoids
SJ 14, SI 9, SI 10 if pain is behind the
armpit
Caution: do not use **LI 4** during pregnancy.

Elbow pain

Repetitive strain injuries of the elbow joint
and surrounding tissues include "tennis
elbow" and "golfer's elbow". Debilitating
elbow pain with tenderness and pain down
the forearm can be caused by supporting
heavy loads across the hands and forearms,
turning the forearm repeatedly, or repetitive
keyboard work. Osteo- and rheumatoid
arthritis are common causes of elbow pain
and immobility in older people. Tui Na
treatment should be daily for at least a week,
and then once a week until the pain has gone
and mobility is restored.

ELBOW PAIN TREATMENT
Apply Tui Na as described in Chapter
Five, Part 2, Step 14 followed by Steps
12–13.

Tennis elbow: pain in the outside of the
elbow, often with extreme tenderness of
the muscles overlying the upper third of
the radius.
LI 10, LI 11
GB 34, LU 5

Golfer's elbow: pain in the inside of the
joint and tenderness in the muscles on the
inside of the upper forearm.
H 3, also *ashi* points (see page 127) on the
muscles on the inner margin of the
forearm.
GB 34, SJ 10, SI 8

Wrist pain

Wrists, in common with elbows, are subject
to repetitive strain injuries, inflammation of
the tendons (tenosynovitis) and, in older
people, arthritic conditions. Carpal tunnel
syndrome is a common wrist problem where
a nerve is compressed where it passes
through the wrist, causing numbness or
tingling in the fingers.

WRIST PAIN TREATMENT
Apply Tui Na as described in Chapter
Five, Part 2, Step 15 to massage and
manipulate the hand and wrist.
P 7, **H 7**, **LU 7**, and *ashi* points
(see page 127).

*Knead deeply around the wrist to stimulate all the
Qi-points on it. If the fingers are numb due to carpal
tunnel syndrome, give particular attention to* **P 7**.

Thumb pain

The causes of thumb pain are similar to those of wrist pain. Use the following treatment in all cases except where there is advanced rheumatoid arthritis in the joints.

THUMB PAIN TREATMENT
Apply Tui Na as described in Chapter Five, Part 2, Step 15. Rotate the thumb vigorously, pull it several times and roll it for 30 seconds between your palms.
LI 4, **LU 10**, and any *ashi* points (see page 127).
Caution: do not use **L1 4** during pregnancy.

Knee pain

Acute knee pain may be caused by a sprain or other injury. Chronic pain can be due to sciatica, degeneration of the cartilage in the joint, and inflamed ligaments. Running on hard roads can cause knee problems, particularly if the feet or ankles are weak.

KNEE PAIN TREATMENT
Apply Tui Na as described in Chapter Five, Part 6, Steps 1, 2, 4–8, and 10.

Pain caused by cartilage and other problems deep inside the knee joint
ST 35 and the other depression on the knee simultaneously and very deeply
ST 34, **ST 36**, **GB 34**
K 10, BL 40

Pain caused by problems with structures of the knee joint such as ligaments or tendons in the knee area
K 10, LV 8
BL 40, BL 57, GB 34, SP 9, SP 10

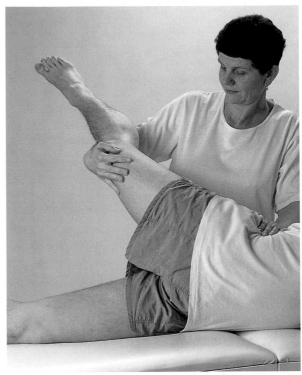

Manipulation of the lower back relieves pain from a rugby injury.

Ankle pain

"Twisted" ankles account for most ankle pain. In older people weakness and chronic pain in the ankles often results from arthritis.

ANKLE PAIN TREATMENT
Apply Tui Na as described in Chapter Five, Part 6, Step 11. Give a full foot massage, emphasizing the ankle rotation and deep kneading across the tendons.

Ankle twisted outward
GB 40
ST 41

Ankle twisted inward
K 3, **K 6**
SP 6
Caution: do not use **SP 6** during pregnancy.

Inflammation of the Achilles tendon
K 3, **BL 60**, and **GB 34**, and squeezing and hacking on the tendon

Deep pain within the ankle joints and general ankle weakness
GB 40, **BL 60**, **K 3**, **K 6**
ST 41, SP 6, K 7
Caution: do not use **SP 6** during pregnancy.

Big toe pain

If not caused by injury, most pain in the big toe, particularly in its basal joint, is probably the result of arthritis. Tightly fitting shoes which may push the big toe out of alignment, will make any joint problem worse.

BIG TOE PAIN TREATMENT
Apply Tui Na as described in Chapter Five, Part 6, with several minutes of big toe rotations and pulls.
LV 3, SP 4

Bruising and sprains

These can occur almost anywhere on the body as the result of trauma. Newly bruised tissue should not be massaged directly.

BRUISING AND SPRAINS TREATMENT
Identify the Meridians that pass through the injured area (see Chapter Three) and deeply knead the Qi-points nearest to, but not on, the damaged tissues. Squeeze and knead sprained areas that are not bruised.

Common ailments

For the following, treat the recommended Qi-points on both sides of the body.

Bronchial asthma

Asthma attacks are recurrent and can vary from mild to life-threatening. Attacks may be triggered by allergens such as pollen, dust, hair, feathers, smoke, and even certain foods. Emotional stress often triggers asthma attack.

BRONCHIAL ASTHMA TREATMENT
Apply Tui Na as described in Chapter Five, Part 7, Steps 7–8, and Part 3, Steps 1–7, massage of the upper back.

For the relief of symptoms
BL 13, **BL 17**, **BL 23**, **R 17**, **LU 7**, **LU 6**, **LU 5**, **ST 36**
GB 21, LI 4, ST 40, LV 14, GB 34, LU 9, LI 10
Caution: do not use **LI 4** during pregnancy.

Constipation

Sluggish action of the colon often results from a diet low in fibre, too little aerobic exercise, or both.

CONSTIPATION TREATMENT
Apply Tui Na as described in Chapter Five, Part 7, Steps 1–6, and abdominal massage with emphasis on deep kneading around the periphery of the abdomen.
Caution: do not massage a pregnant woman on the abdomen.

ST 25, **ST 36**
LI 4, BL 25
Caution: do not use **LI 4** during pregnancy.

Diarrhoea

Acute diarrhoea resulting from contaminated food or water does not normally last for more than two or three days. If there is a sudden change of bowel habit to one of persistent diarrhoea, consult a doctor.

DIARRHOEA TREATMENT
Apply Tui Na as described in Chapter Five, Part 7, Steps 1–6, abdominal massage.

ST 25, SP 9, ST 36, R 6, K 16
BL 23, BL 25, BL 32

Headaches and migraine

The immediate cause of headache pain is usually disturbance of the blood flow through the meninges (the membranes that cover the brain), which changes the pressure through them. Mild headaches vary from a feeling of heaviness to a persistent dull ache, while more severe headaches may bring deep, sharp, or throbbing pains. Headache pain may be felt all over the head (general), at the base of the skull (occipital), on the forehead (frontal), on the temples (temporal), or on the sides of the head (lateral).

Some headaches result from a stimulus such as alcohol, or a hot, stuffy atmosphere, persistent loud noise, thundery weather, or hunger. Those caused by tension, particularly in the neck, are most common, and can recur as long as the cause of stress remains unchecked. If headaches are persistent and do not respond to Tui Na, consult a doctor.

Migraines are severe headaches, often accompanied by visual disturbances, nausea, vomiting, or vertigo, and can last for several days. Treat with Tui Na every few hours.

HEADACHE AND MIGRAINE TREATMENT
Apply Tui Na as described in Chapter Five, Part 1, Steps 1–7 followed by Part 8, Steps 1–9, massage of the face and scalp.

Headache at the base of the skull (occipital)
GB 20, BL 10, GB 21, BL 60
LI 4, LU 7
Caution: do not use **LI 4** during pregnancy.

Headache at the front of the head and/or ache around the eyes
LI 4, GB 20, GB 14
GB 21, BL 2, Yintang, ST 41
Caution: do not use **LI 4** during pregnancy.

Headache at the side of the head and/or on the temples
Taiyang, GB 20, GB 21, SJ 3, SJ 5
GB 8, LI 4
Caution: do not use **LI 4** during pregnancy.

Headache at the top of the head
LV 3, D 20

Migraine with nausea and vomiting
P 6, ST 36, BL 17
Other points according to where the pain manifests, as above.

Insomnia

Sleeplessness can take several different forms: difficulty in getting to sleep because of an active mind; shallow sleep disturbed by dreams, or waking in the night and being unable to get back to sleep. Tui Na for the neck, shoulder, back, and face are particularly effective.

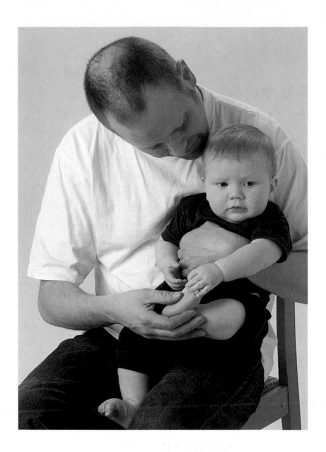

Tui Na treatments for babies and young children work on Qi-points of the feet and hands.

INSOMNIA TREATMENT

Apply Tui Na as described in Chapter Five, Part 8, Steps 1–12.

SP 6, **ST 36**, **H 7**, **P 6**, **P 8**, **Yintang, K 1**
LV 3

Caution: do not use **SP 6** during pregnancy.

Irritable bowel syndrome

This condition is frequently stress-related. Symptoms include abdominal pain and indigestion, erratic bowel habit with diarrhoea or constipation, or both.

IBS TREATMENT

Apply Tui Na as described in Chapter Five, Part 7, Steps 1–5.

ST 25, **R 6**, **R 12**, **ST 36**, **SP 6**, **LI 4**, **K 16**
BL 20, BL 21, BL 25, LI 10, LI 11, BL 32

Caution: do not use **SP 6** or **LI 4** during pregnancy.

Sinusitis

Sinusitis is an inflammation of the facial sinuses, usually caused by infection. There may be a congested or blocked nose, pressure around the eyes, often accompanied by a throbbing ache, and loss of the sense of smell.

SINUSITIS TREATMENT

Apply Tui Na as described in Chapter Five, Part 1, Steps 5–6, and Part 8, Steps 1–9. This treatment also relieves rhinitis caused by allergies.

LI 4, **LI 20**, **Yintang**
BL 2, LU 5

Caution: do not use **LI 4** during pregnancy.

Tui Na for infants

Massage for children under the age of five is a specialized branch of Tui Na and is widely practised in China. It is effective in treating non-infectious conditions, and boosts the immune system, as well as stimulating full physical and mental development. Three effective techniques for common conditions are described here.

Infants will only accept Tui Na if they enjoy and feel comfortable with the feelings it gives them. On the first few occasions only use very light pressure, increasing it gradually as the child adapts.

RUBBING AROUND THE *NEIBAGUA*

If you imagine the palm to be a saucer, the *neibagua* is a circle found midway between the periphery of the base and the rim. Its centre is Qi-point **P 8**. A good time to use this technique is just before bedtime. Use some baby talcum powder on the skin and start the massage with gentle kneading of **P 8**. Use very small circular movements and knead at least 50 times. Now rub clockwise around the *neibagua*, making 50–100 circles. Repeat on the other hand.

BENEFITS:
This treatment promotes the flow of blood and Qi and stimulates the Zang–Fu (see page 17). It is powerfully soothing for the baby who cries a great deal during the night. Rub anti-clockwise to treat wind, diarrhoea, and vomiting.

STIMULATING **ST 36**

Use the pad of the thumb to knead this point at the side of the knee, starting with very light pressure as it is likely to be very sensitive. Press and knead at least 50 times and then repeat on the other leg.

BENEFITS:
This treatment soothes abdominal pain, treats loose bowel action, and boosts immunity.

RUBBING THE ABDOMEN

Use the palm to rub clockwise around the abdomen between the navel and pubic bone in the area of **R 6**. Make between 30 and 50 circling movements.

BENEFITS:
This treatment is excellent for restlessness. It eases constipation, strengthens the Spleen and Stomach, and promotes healthy functioning of the digestive tract.

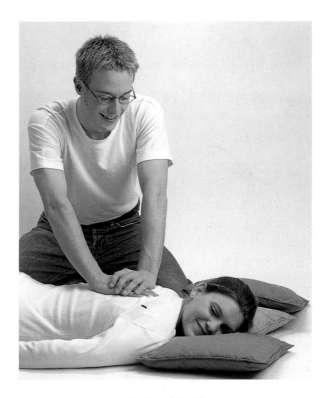

Kneading along the Bladder Meridian relaxes an aching back caused by sitting at a desk for long periods.

Tui Na in adolescence

Adolescence is the period of physical, mental, and emotional change and maturation that marks the change from childhood to adulthood. Adolescents may experience difficulties in their relationships both inside and outside the family, with developing an adult identity, and with trying to reconcile their own desires with the expectations of parents and society. Many are taking exams and having to make important career choices. The emotions may tend to dominate life at this stage, especially anger and anxiety.

The typical physical problems of adolescence are usually due to hormonal imbalance and lifestyle. Teenage acne, poor concentration, and anaemia all result from excesses (in "fast food", worry, and late nights) and deficiencies (in nutritious food, relaxation, or sleep). Tui Na is excellent for many adolescent conditions because it treats both the emotional and physical causes.

ADOLESCENTS' TREATMENT
Neck, shoulder, and back massage is good for those who are stressed from living life at top speed. See elsewhere in this chapter for treatments for constipation, insomnia, and other conditions. Use the *Shu* points on the Bladder Meridian of the back (see page 24) to strengthen the Organs.

Anxiety and worry
SP 6, P 6
K 3, K 1, Yintang
Caution: do not use **SP 6** during pregnancy.

Lack of concentration
SP 6, ST 36, D 20, BL 23
Caution: do not use **SP 6** during pregnancy.

Anger and rebelliousness
LV 3, P 6, Yintang

Acne
SP 6, SP 10, LI 11, ST 36
Caution: do not use **SP 6** during pregnancy.

Red and/or shadowy eyes
SJ 23, BL 2, LI 4, LV 3
Caution: do not use **LI 4** during pregnancy.

PMT
R 6, SP 6, LV 3, H 7 or P 6, ST 36
LI 4, Taiyang
Caution: do not use **SP 6** or **LI 4** during pregnancy.

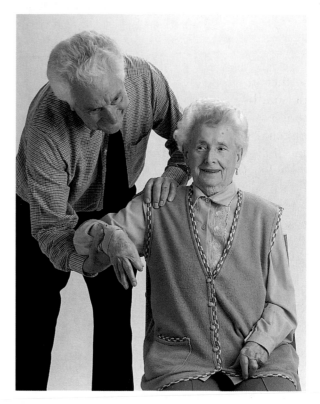

A gentle arm rotation loosens an arthritic shoulder joint, relieving pain and increasing flexibility.

Tui Na in the later years

According to Chinese theory, the problems associated with ageing are due to a deficiency of Qi, which decreases as we grow older. Disharmonies in Qi may also develop, which make us more prone to bronchial and chest problems, feeling cold, poor hearing and ringing in the ears (tinnitus), frequency of urination, retention of urine, or incontinence. High blood pressure is especially common among older people. Causes include narrowing of the arteries and stress; the condition is made worse by obesity, smoking, excess alcohol, and a very sedentary lifestyle.

The ageing process cannot be stopped, but it can be slowed and balanced using Tui Na. People in their late eighties can benefit from and enjoy Tui Na just as much as those in their thirties. When massaging an elderly person, bear in mind that joints become less mobile with age, and lying face down may be difficult, so you may have to give treatments in other positions. Be aware that older people have less body fat, and less "padding" on the bones, and the soft tissues are often tender and can bruise very easily. Also, do not treat anyone with osteoporosis or brittle bones.

TREATMENT IN THE LATER YEARS

The neck, shoulders, arms, and back should be massaged unless specifically contraindicated (see page 12).

High blood pressure (hypertension)
GB 20, LV 3, P 6, H 7, ST 36, LI 11, BL 15
K 1, LI 4, P 7, P 3
Caution: do not use **LI 4** during pregnancy.
Blood pressure tends to fall during Tui Na treatment, whether or not there is high blood pressure.

Heart problems
BL 15, BL 13, H 7

Enlarged or inflamed prostate gland. Difficulty in passing urine, with or without lower abdominal pain
SP 6, R 3
R 6, SP 9, ST 36
Caution: do not use **SP 6** during pregnancy.

For general wellbeing stimulate these Health Care points (see page 24) as often as possible
GB 20, GB 21, GB 30, ST 36, LI 4, LI 10, LI 11, LI 20, LU 7, P 6 or **H 7, K 1, SP 6, LV 3, BL 2, BL 23, R 3, R 6**
Caution: do not use **L1 4** or **SP 6** during pregnancy.

Daily Tui Na self-treatment

Everyone can benefit from a daily Tui Na session. The best method is to pummel all the accessible parts of the body and knead the essential Qi-points. If you make this a daily routine, you will boost your "feel good" factor and slow down the ageing process.

Start pummelling with your right hand up the outside of your left arm to the shoulder and then down the inside. Repeat several times. Then work with your left hand on the right arm. Support your right elbow with your left hand as you pummel across the top of the left shoulder reaching **GB 21** if possible. Repeat on the other side.

Using both hands pummel the front of the chest particularly in the region of the Qi-points **LU 1** and **LU 2**. From standing, bend forward and pummel down both sides of the back and buttocks to stimulate the Bladder Meridian and **GB 30**. Then using the heels of both hands, vigorously rub **BL 23** to stimulate the Kidney.

Remaining in the forward leaning position, move the legs apart and pummel down the outside and then up the inside of both the legs simultaneously. Lift one leg on to a chair, as high as is comfortable and pummel with both hands up and down. Repeat for the other leg.

Press and knead these Health Care points
GB 20, GB 21, ST 36, LI 4, LI 11, LI 20, LU 7, P 6, K 1, K 3, SP 6, Taiyang, Yintang, LV 3, BL 2, BL 23, R 6, D 20
Caution: do not use **LI 4** and **SP 6** during pregnancy.

Appendix

The *cun* measurement

The *cun* is a non-standard unit, used in Chinese Medicine to measure the distance of Qi-points from body "landmarks", such as bones and muscles (see below and right).

The width of the thumb is 1 *cun*; the combined width of the index and middle finger is 1.5 *cun*; and the four fingers together make 3 *cun*. Clearly the *cun* varies from one person to another. You need to use the width of your partner's own fingers to give you their *cun* measurement in order to locate their Qi-points accurately.

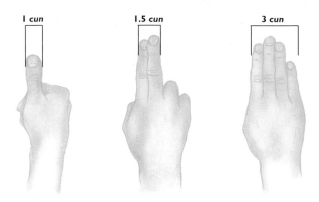

The muscles

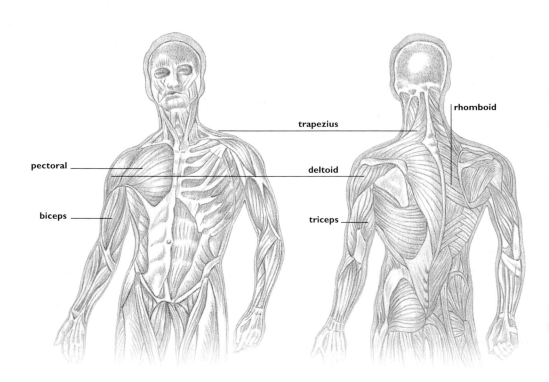

The bones

The vertebrae of the spine and the ribs are counted down from the top of the body. For example, the 3rd rib is the third one down. Bones on the hands are counted outward from the bone nearest the thumb. For the feet, count outward from the bone nearest the big toe.

To locate vertebrae, use these landmarks: cervical vertebra 7 is the prominent vertebra on the back of the neck when the head is bent forward; the soft part of the waist is level with the gap between lumbar vertebrae 2 and 3.

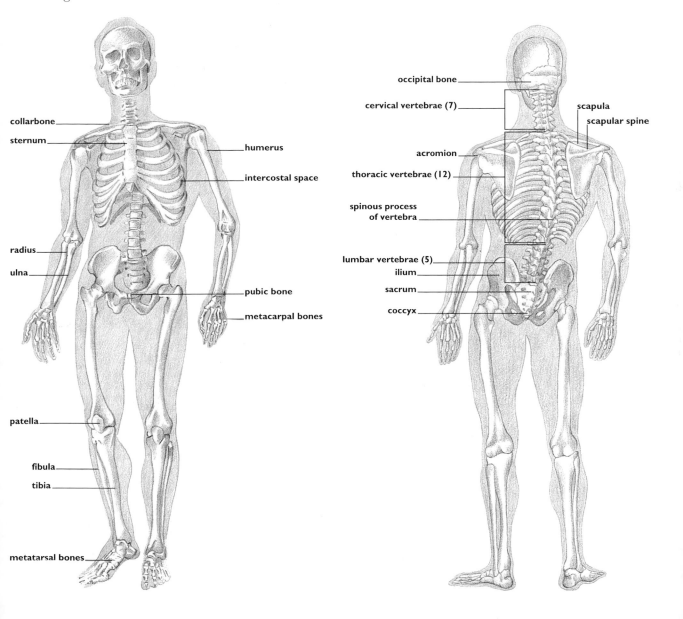

collarbone
sternum
humerus
intercostal space
radius
ulna
pubic bone
metacarpal bones
patella
fibula
tibia
metatarsal bones

occipital bone
cervical vertebrae (7)
scapula
scapular spine
acromion
thoracic vertebrae (12)
spinous process of vertebra
lumbar vertebrae (5)
ilium
sacrum
coccyx

Glossary

Achilles tendon tendon connecting the calf muscles to the heelbone

acute describes a sudden, intense condition that may be of short duration

adipose fatty

bursitis inflammation of a bursa, a small fluid-filled sac between joints

cartilage gristle on the surfaces of bones in the joints

cervical of the neck

cervical spondylitis inflammation of the neck vertebrae

chafe to rub the skin; see p. 60

chiropractic treatment of disorders through manipulation, especially of the spine

chronic describes a persistent and debilitating condition

conjunctivitis inflammation of the eye membranes

connective tissue cells supporting and connecting organs, also tendons and ligaments

cun a non-standard measurement; see p. 138

cupping a percussive technique; see p. 67

deltoid the thick muscle on the outer edge of the shoulder

Du Meridian; see p. 51

eczema skin inflammation with scaly, itching, or burning lesions

fibrositis inflammation of fibrous tissue, especially around muscles

fibula the thin outer bone of the lower leg

hack to strike with the edge of the hand; see p. 66

hamstring the tendon at the back of the knee

humerus the upper arm bone

ilio-sacral describes the region joining the sacrum and ilium; see p. 139

ligament fibre linking bone and cartilage

lumbago pain in the lower back

lumbar the region between the lowest ribs and the hipbones

Meridian a channel through which Qi flows

metacarpal hand bone between wrist and knuckes

midline the central line of the body, viewed front or back

neuralgia severe pain along one or more nerves

occipital of the back of the head or skull

osteoarthritis degenerative condition of the joints with pain and stiffness

osteopathy a system of healing based on manipulation, particularly of the bones

osteoporosis a condition where the bones become porous and brittle, due to calcium loss

palmar of the palm of the hand

pectoral large chest muscle that moves the shoulder and upper arm

percussion striking or hitting; see p. 66

Pericardium an Organ closely linked to the Heart

pluck to pull across muscled tissue; see p. 63

PMT pre-menstrual tension; also called pre-menstrual syndrome

prolapse sinking of an organ or part from its normal position

psoriasis skin disease with reddish, scaly, itching patches

pummel to strike the skin with loose fists; see p. 66

Qi vital energy or life force which flows in Meridians

Qi-point point on a Meridian where Qi can be manipulated

radius the outer bone of the lower arm

Ren Meridian; see p. 50

rheumatoid arthritis a chronic disease of the musculo-skeletal system, with joint inflammation, swelling, and pain

rhinitis inflammation of the nose membranes

rhomboid muscle between the spine and the shoulder

sacrum wedge-shaped bone at the base of the spine see p. 139

scapula the triangular back shoulder bone see p. 139

sciatica neuralgia of the sciatic nerve, which runs down the leg

sclerosis hardening or thickening of tissues

sinusitis inflammation of the sinuses

spinous process the outward bony protrusion of a vertebra

tendon fibrous tissue joining muscle to bone

thoracic of the thorax, the area between the neck and the lumbar region

tinnitus ringing in the ears

trapezius flat triangular muscle on the side of the back, shoulders, and neck; see p. 138

ulna the inner, longer bone of the lower arm

urticaria hives, or nettle rash

yin and **yang** two aspects of the underlying principle of Chinese philosophy; see p.15.

Resources

There are as yet very few qualified Tui Na therapists in the West. For a Register of qualified Tui Na practitioners, or for information on Tui Na training courses, write to:

BODYHARMONICS® Centre
54 Flecker's Drive
Hatherley
Cheltenham GL51 5BD
England

> The video cassette *Step-by-Step Tui Na* demonstrates many of the techniques and the basic routines used in *The Handbook of Chinese Massage*. Send $25 plus $5 package and mailing to the BODYHARMONICS® Centre at the above address.

Further Reading

Chaitow, Leon. *The Acupuncture Treatment of Pain.* Healing Arts Press, 1990.

Chaitow, Leon. *Soft-Tissue Manipulation.* Healing Arts Press, 1988.

Dubitsky, Carl. *BodyWork Shiatsu.* Healing Arts Press, 1997.

Fan Ya-li. *Chinese Pediatric Massage Therapy.* Blue Poppy Press, 1994.

Kenyon, Julian. *Acupressure Techniques.* Healing Arts Press, 1988.

Seem, Mark. *Acupuncture Energetics.* Healing Arts Press, 1987.

Seem, Mark. *Acupuncture Imaging.* Healing Arts Press, 1990.

Sohn, Tina and Robert. *Amma Therapy.* Healing Arts Press, 1996.

Wills, Pauline. *The Reflexology Manual.* Healing Arts Press, 1995.

Author's acknowledgements

I owe a debt of gratitude to the Chinese doctors of the Traditional Chinese hospitals of Shanghai, Weihai, and X'ian who have most generously and patiently taught me the theory and practice of Tui Na. In particular, I give special thanks to Dr Zhao Shui-an who has given unstintingly of his time, expertise, and care during each of my five visits.

My thanks also go to my husband Trevor for the enjoyable hours of discussion and brainstorming involved in preparing this book, and to my daughters Gisela, Gina, and Danella, and my son Graham, for patiently and skilfully modelling for most of the photographs and being excellent ambassadors for Tui Na.

Lastly a special word of thanks to Lucy for the long hours of work she has spent designing the book, and to Caroline, the editor for simplifying the sophisticated text and making it easily understood.

Publisher's acknowledgements

Many thanks to Jenny and Owen Dixon for the computer generated artwork.

The publishers would also like to thank Lynn Bresler for the index; and the following who posed for photographs in this book: Maria Mercati and her family, Jamie Dawkins, Neal Wickens, Phil and Alexander Johnson, Gertrude Mercati, John Hellier, and Frank Forbes.

All artwork was by Aziz Khan, except pages 21, 25, 27, 32, 37, 42, 45, and 138–9.

Index